Presented to

_____

From

_____

Date

_____

An Eager Reader Devotional

GOD IS GREAT

Edited by
Daryl J. Lucas

Illustrated by
Daniel J. Hochstatter

CONTRIBUTORS
Betsy Rossen Elliot, Joey O'Conner
Mark Fackler, Mary Ann Lackland
and Len Woods

**TYNDALE
FOR KIDS**

This book was produced with the assistance of The Livingstone Corporation.

All Scripture quotations are taken from *The Simplified Living Bible*, copyright © 1990 by KNT Charitable Trust. Used by permission of Tyndale House Publishers, Inc. All rights reserved.

Library of Congress Cataloging-in-Publication Data

Printed in the United States of America

01 00 99 98 97 96 95
7 6 5 4 3 2 1

TIPS FOR PARENTS

God Is Great: An Eager Reader Devotional has been designed to spark conversation between you and your young child (or children). Older children may enjoy reading the stories themselves, or you may want to read them aloud. The reference for the corresponding Bible passage for each devotional is given right below the title. (Some of the stories also appear in *The Eager Reader Bible*. When that is the case, the page number is given at the bottom of the page.) Whether your child reads the story alone or you do it together, you should try to be available to talk with them about the questions.

Here are a few things I've learned from the way devotions work (and don't work!) in my own family, which may help you get the most out of your family devotions times:

(1) When you ask a question, wait a while before moving on to the next one. Give your child time to think of an answer—or several answers. They may not answer right away, but that's OK. If you move on too quickly, they won't be as willing to ponder your questions, and you'll miss some of the ideas

that would come to them after a bit of thought.

(2) Try several different times of day to see what works best for your family. Many families like to use dinnertime for family devotions. Others prefer bedtime. I prefer bedtime because my kids are more interested in talking then than they are at meals. During meals they are distracted by their eating and their thoughts about other things. But at bedtime, discussing the Scriptures and the questions is a nice excuse to stay up a little longer. And I have their undivided attention.

(3) Do not underestimate your child's willingness to sit and listen to a Bible story. Every child is different, but many children will sit and listen to a good story even if it is quite long. Try reading long portions of the Bible to your kids. You may find that they follow along just fine!

Finding the best time, setting, and format for your devotional times with young children will require flexibility and a bit of experimenting. But it's worth every effort it takes to make this a time your child will enjoy and look forward to.

Daryl J. Lucas

CONTENTS

AN EAGER READER DEVOTIONAL

GOD IS GREAT

Treat People with Respect
GENESIS 1—2

God made man like his Maker. Like God did God make man. Man and maid did he make them.

GENESIS 1:27

You can read more about how God made everything on page 14 of *The Eager Reader Bible*.

God made the oceans and all kinds of fish. He made the animals that live on the land, too— even the bugs. But God saved the best part for last. After he made everything else, he made people. Every single person is a very special creation. Treat all people with respect. Don't call them names or hit them. They need to be treated special, just like you.

1. How did God make Adam and Eve special?
2. Why is it bad to call people names or hit them or treat them badly?
3. Who treats YOU with respect? How?

Dear God,
*   I am glad that you made people. Please help me to treat others with respect. Amen.*

Take Care of the Earth
GENESIS 1:28

God blessed them and told them, "Multiply and fill the earth and subdue it. You are masters of the fish and birds and all the animals."

GENESIS 1:28

Would you like to share a home with lions and giraffes? Adam and Eve did. They lived with these creatures in God's garden. God told Adam and Eve to take good care of the earth and all of its animals. He put them in charge of it all. Now WE are in charge of the earth. God has put you and every other person in charge of the lions and the giraffes and everything else. Keep the earth clean and beautiful. Take care of all its creatures!

1. What are your favorite animals? fish? birds?
2. What would happen to the earth if we did not take care of it?
3. What can you and your family do to keep your town clean?

Dear God,
    Thank you for making the earth so beautiful. Help me to take good care of it all. Amen.

Obeying God
GENESIS 3

**Obey God because you are his children.
Don't slip back into your old ways. For then
you did evil because you didn't know better.**

1 PETER 1:14

You can read more about the very first sin on
page 18 of *The Eager Reader Bible*.

God gave Adam and Eve a beautiful garden to live in. The only thing God wanted them to do was obey him. Obeying him is all Adam and Eve had to do. "Everything in the whole garden is yours," God said. "The only thing you can't do is eat the fruit on this one tree." Adam and Eve did not obey God. They both ate the fruit that God said not to eat. So Adam and Eve had to leave God's garden forever. It's always best to do what God says.

1. What are some of the rules you have to obey?
2. When do you think it's hard to obey God?
3. Why is it important to obey God?

Dear God,
Your rules are important, but sometimes I forget. Please forgive me when I don't obey you. I know you will always let me try again. Amen.

Loving God
GENESIS 6

Noah did all that God told him.

GENESIS 6:22

You can read more about Noah and the ark
on page 22 of *The Eager Reader Bible*.

Noah loved God. That's why Noah obeyed God. Everyone else did whatever they wanted, but Noah did things that God wanted him to do. When God told Noah to build a huge boat, Noah went right to work. Building the ark took a long time. It was hard work. But Noah wanted to please God, so he sawed those boards and built that boat. And when the flood came, Noah and his family were safe—the only people on earth to live through the terrible flood. God takes care of people who love and obey him.

1. What do you like best about the story of Noah and the ark?
2. What are some of God's commands in the Bible?
3. When is it hard to obey God?

Dear God,
Please help me to be like Noah. I want to do whatever you command. Amen.

[God said to Noah,] "I will see the rainbow in the cloud. And I will remember my eternal promise to every living being on the earth."

GENESIS 9:16-17

You can read more about the big flood on page 26 of *The Eager Reader Bible.*

Have you ever been afraid in a thunderstorm? Think what Noah and the animals felt like. For 40 days they had to stay indoors. So much rain, lightning, and thunder must have been pretty scary. When the rain finally stopped, the ark settled on a mountaintop. Then God made a promise: Never again will the whole earth flood like that. The rainbow in the sky helps us remember that God always keeps his promises.

1. What makes it hard to keep promises?
2. What promises has God made to you?
3. How do you know God will keep his promises?

Dear God,
Thank you for promising us eternal life in heaven. I believe you. Amen.

The Lord appeared to Abram and said, "I am going to give this land to your descendants." And Abram built an altar there to the Lord.

GENESIS 12:7

You can read more about Abram and Sarai
on page 30 of *The Eager Reader Bible.*

One day God told Abram and Sarai to leave their home and go far away. Abram and Sarai knew they had been chosen by God. So they went. Abram and Sarai did not know what would happen in their new home. But they knew God, and they trusted him. Finally they got to their new land. And one of the first things they did was set up a special place for worshiping God called an altar. They knew that worship is very important.

1. How do you know that worshiping God was important to Abram and Sarai?
2. What do you usually do to worship God?
3. What different ways can people worship God?

Dear God,
    You are a mighty God. Please help me to remember to praise and worship you like Abram and Sarai. Amen.

Stop Arguing!
GENESIS 13

Abram talked it over with Lot. "This fighting between our men has got to stop," he said. "We can't afford to let a rift develop between our clans. Close relatives such as we are must be united!"

GENESIS 13:8

You can read more about Abram and Lot on page 34 of *The Eager Reader Bible*.

Abram and Lot were in the same family. Abram was Lot's uncle. But their families and workers argued a lot. They all wanted to live in the same place. Somebody had to move. But who? Abram decided to stop the argument and give Lot first choice of the land. Abram loved his nephew Lot. He knew that showing love to your family is more important than winning an argument.

1. What do you think about what Abram did for Lot?
2. What do you argue about in your family?
3. How could you work it out the next time you and your brother or sister (or friend) want the same thing?

> *Dear God,*
> *Thank you for my family. Please help me to talk things out instead of arguing and fighting. Amen.*

Being First
GENESIS 13

[Abram said,] "I'll tell you what we'll do. Choose any section of land you want. I will take what's left. If you want that part over there to the east, then I'll stay here in the west. Or, if you want the west, then I'll go over there to the east."

GENESIS 13:9

Abram and Lot had a problem. They had big herds of goats and sheep. They had so many animals that their shepherds began to quarrel and fight over the grass the animals were eating. The shepherds didn't know how to think of others first. Abram had a great idea. He told Lot that all they had to do was divide up the land. Then he said, "You can have the land you want. You choose first." Abram thought of Lot first. That settled the whole problem.

1. What makes you angry about stingy people?
2. Why is it important to share?
3. What is hard about sharing with others?

Dear Lord,
*   Thank you for always thinking of me first. Please help me to share and think of others first, too. Amen.*

God Can Do Neat Things
GENESIS 17, 21

Then God did as he had promised. Sarah became pregnant and gave Abraham a baby son in his old age. And it happened at the time God had said.

GENESIS 21:1-2

You can read more about Isaac's birth on page 42 of *The Eager Reader Bible.*

The name *Isaac* means "laughter." Why would Abraham and Sarah name their son "laughter"? It was because of the miracle. Abraham was 99 years old. Sarah was 89. Even though God had promised long before to give them a baby, they thought they were too old to be parents. They had been waiting a long time, and nothing had happened. But God can do anything. When Isaac was born, Abraham and Sarah were filled with joy. They laughed because they were happy. They learned that God can do anything.

1. What do you like best about the story of Isaac?
2. Why is it so hard to wait for things that you really want?
3. God can do anything. What is something you wish God would do?

Dear God,
I'm so glad you can do anything. Nothing is too hard for you. Amen.

A Rescue Story
GENESIS 19:1-29

"Sirs," [Lot] said, "come to my home. Be my guests for the night. You can get up as early as you like and be on your way again."

GENESIS 19:2

You can read more about Lot and his guests on page 38 of *The Eager Reader Bible*.

Two angels came to the city where Lot lived. Lot thought that the angels were men. So he invited them to stay at his house. He wanted them to have dinner and to spend the night. Evil men came to Lot's house. They tried to barge in. But Lot would not let them in. "Leave my guests alone," Lot said. "This is a safe house." Lot and his guests barred the door. Together they got the evil men to leave them alone. Who says bullies should always get their way?

1. What do bullies do to bug other kids?
2. What do you wish you could do to stop bullies?
3. What should you do the next time a bully starts picking on other kids?

Dear God,
    I want to be a defender. Please help me and other kids to protect each other. Amen.

Manners
GENESIS 19:1-29

"Oh no, sirs, please," Lot begged. . . . "Let me flee to that little town over there."

GENESIS 19:18

Lot and his family lived in the city of Sodom. But God was going to destroy the city because of all the bad things people were doing there. So God sent angels to get Lot and his family to safety. The angels said, "Run to the mountains!" But Lot felt scared about moving into the wilderness. "Please," he begged, "let me go instead to that nearby city." And the angel granted Lot's polite request. Lot had good manners. Do you?

1. Why do you think Lot said please?
2. Why are manners important?
3. How do you feel when someone forgets to say please?

> *Dear God,*
> *I want to have good manners. Please help me to remember to be polite when I talk to others. Amen.*

Pray When You're Stumped

"This evening when I came to the spring I prayed this prayer: 'O Lord, the God of my master Abraham. Please make my mission a success. Please guide me in this way.'"

GENESIS 24:42

It was time for Isaac to start his own family. So his father, Abraham, sent a trusted helper on a long journey. "Find a woman who can marry Isaac," he said. The helper set out. But how do you find someone you've never met in a place you've never been? The helper knew what to do. He prayed. And God helped him find Rebekah. Whenever you don't know what to do, pray. Ask God for wisdom. He will help you see the way!

1. What made the helper's job really hard?
2. What's one of the hardest jobs you have ever done?
3. When you think about growing up, what do you want God to help you decide?

> *Dear God,*
> *Growing up means facing a lot of decisions. Please remind me to ask for wisdom whenever I'm stumped. Amen.*

Not So Fast!
GENESIS 25:19-34

Then Jacob gave Esau bread, peas, and stew. So he ate and drank and went on about his business. He did not seem to care that he had thrown away his birthright.

GENESIS 25:34

You can read more about Jacob and Esau on page 50 of *The Eager Reader Bible.*

Isaac gave his son Esau a gift called a *birthright*. It meant that someday Esau would get all that his father owned. It was a very special gift because only one son could have it. One day Esau came home very hungry. Jacob was cooking stew, and Esau wanted some. Esau was so hungry that he traded his birthright for some stew. Pretty soon Esau was sorry he had traded. But Jacob had gotten the birthright fair and square. Esau learned the hard way not to do things without thinking about them first.

1. What are some of the best gifts you ever got?
2. Why do you think Esau was so quick to trade away his special gift?
3. When do you need to be on your guard against quick and easy choices?

> *Dear God,*
>   *Sometimes I feel like I have to do something right now, like Esau did. Please teach me to think about it first. Amen.*

Honesty
GENESIS 27

A good person hates lies. Wicked people lie all the time and soon come to shame.

PROVERBS 13:5

You can read more about about Jacob and Esau on page 50 of *The Eager Reader Bible*.

Jacob had one thing on his mind. He wanted his father's blessing. And he was even willing to tell a lie to get it. It was easy to trick his father, Isaac. Jacob knew in his heart that he should not pretend to be his twin brother. But he did it anyway. He lied to his father and said he was Esau. That lie caused many problems in their family for years and years. God wants us always to tell the truth.

1. When is it easy to lie? Why?
2. What do you think Jacob should have done about wanting Esau's blessing?
3. What bad things can happen when somebody lies?

Dear God,
    Sometimes it is easy to lie. But you love the truth. Please help me always to tell the truth. Amen.

God Is with You
GENESIS 28:10-22

[God said] "Always remember that I am with you. I will protect you wherever you go. And I will bring you back safely to this land. I will be with you always until I have finished giving you all I am promising."

GENESIS 28:15

You can read more about Jacob leaving home on page 58 of *The Eager Reader Bible*.

Jacob and his brother, Esau, got into a big fight. Esau was very angry. Esau wanted to hurt Jacob. So their mother, Rebekah, sent Jacob away. Jacob's journey was long. Jacob needed God's help. He became very tired and lay down to sleep. That night God spoke to Jacob in a dream. God promised always to be with Jacob. He would help Jacob every day. Jacob learned that God would be with him wherever he went. And God will always be with you, too.

1. What is your favorite part of the story of Jacob?
2. How did God help Jacob?
3. When do you want to ask God for help?

Dear Lord,
Thank you for being with me every day. Please teach me to trust you whenever I am afraid. Amen.

Forgiveness
GENESIS 32-33

Then Esau ran to meet [Jacob] and hugged him and kissed him. Both of them were in tears!

GENESIS 33:4

You can read more about Esau forgiving Jacob on page 62 of *The Eager Reader Bible.*

Would you be angry if someone took something of yours? Esau was angry. His brother Jacob had taken his birthright and blessing. Esau was so angry that he had wanted to kill his brother! Jacob even ran away from home to get away. Over time, God taught Esau a lesson. God showed Esau that he needed to forgive Jacob. So Esau did forgive Jacob. And the brothers who used to fight and argue hugged and became friends again. Good friends don't stay mad forever.

1. Why do you think it was hard for Esau to forgive Jacob?
2. When do kids need to forgive each other?
3. Who is someone you need to forgive?

Dear God,
Thank you for forgiving me when I do wrong. Help me to forgive others too. Amen.

Don't Boast or Brag
Genesis 37:1-36

"So you want to be our king, do you?" his brothers derided. And they hated him both for the dream and for his cocky attitude.

GENESIS 37:8

You can read more about Joseph and his brothers on page 66 of *The Eager Reader Bible.*

Nobody likes friends who brag all the time. That's what Joseph's brothers thought Joseph was like. And they were right. Joseph did brag too much. So they decided to teach him a lesson. First they said they would kill him. But they calmed down and only threw him into a pit. Then they sold him to merchants to get rid of him for good. That was a pretty hard lesson, but Joseph sure learned not to brag.

1. What do you brag about?
2. What's a good way to help a friend stop bragging?
3. What can you do when you want to brag?

Dear God,
    Help me not to brag. When I feel like a champion, I'll just do my best to help others. Amen.

She kept on asking day after day. Joseph refused to listen. He kept out of her way as much as possible.

GENESIS 39:10

J oseph liked his boss, Potiphar. But Potiphar's wife was sneaky and mean. One day she wanted Joseph to do something bad. Joseph said no. He would not even be around Potiphar's wife anymore. She got angry with Joseph. She told lies about Joseph to get him in trouble. But God knew Joseph had done nothing wrong. He made good things happen to Joseph because Joseph did what was right.

1. When was a time someone asked you to do something bad?
2. What's one of the best ways to say no to someone who wants you to do something bad?
3. What can you do if a friend asks you to do something wrong?

Dear God,
  Thank you for telling me about right and wrong. Help me to say no when people tell me to do bad things. Amen.

Remember People Who Help You
GENESIS 40–41

Pharaoh's wine taster, however, forgot all about Joseph. He never gave him another thought.

GENESIS 40:23

You can read more about Joseph on page 66 of *The Eager Reader Bible.*

When Joseph was in prison, he helped the king's wine taster. The wine taster promised to remember Joseph when he got out of prison. Then maybe the king would let Joseph out, too. But the wine taster forgot Joseph. After two years, the wine taster remembered Joseph and told the king about him. Joseph was let out of prison and became a great leader. Remember to help the people who do nice things for you.

1. What helps you to remember your promises?
2. What nice thing has someone done for you lately?
3. What could you do to show and tell nice people that you are thankful?

Dear God,
   Thank you for my family and friends. Please help me remember all the nice things they do for me. Amen.

Forgiveness
GENESIS 42—45

[Joseph said,] "God has sent me here to
keep you and your families alive."

GENESIS 45:7

You can read more about Joseph forgiving his
brothers on page 78 of *The Eager Reader Bible.*

When Joseph was young, his older brothers were very jealous of him. His brothers were so mean to him that they even tried to kill him. Joseph's brothers sold him to some merchants, and Joseph became a slave. Years later, Joseph became a very important person in Egypt. But he missed his brothers. He still loved them. When he saw them again, he said, "It's OK. I forgive you." Even though his brothers had been mean to him, Joseph forgave his brothers. That's what God's people always try to do.

1. Why was Joseph nice to his mean brothers?
2. What makes it hard to be nice to a mean person?
3. When someone is mean to you, what does God want you to do?

Dear Jesus,
Sometimes people are mean to me. Please help me to forgive them. Amen.

Serving God
EXODUS 1—2

[The princess] named him Moses (meaning "to draw out") because she had drawn him out of the water.

EXODUS 2:10

You can read more about baby Moses on page 82 of *The Eager Reader Bible.*

In the story of Moses, God used a simple basket as a little boat. God used a princess to find the basket-boat with Moses in it. God used a big sister to help the princess find someone to feed the baby. God used a mommy to feed the baby. If God can use a basket and a sister and a mommy, he can also use you. Isn't that neat? God wants to use you to do great things!

1. Why would it be hard to hide a baby?
2. How do you think the family of Moses felt when they put their baby into a floating basket? Why?
3. How would you like to be used by God?

Dear God,
    You are so great, you can use anyone or anything. Please use me today to do your will. Amen.

When You're Scared
EXODUS 2:23—4:20

"But I'm not the person for a job like that!"
Moses exclaimed. Then God told him, "I
really will be with you."

EXODUS 3:11-12

You can read more about when God told Moses
to help on page 86 of *The Eager Reader Bible.*

Moses was pretty brave, but sometimes he got scared. It was hard for him to admit, but Moses was afraid to give public speeches. And he was REALLY afraid to tell the king of Egypt that all the Hebrew slaves had to leave. "WHAT?" Pharaoh would scream. "Lose my slaves? Never!" So God sent Moses a helper—his brother, Aaron. That would help him not to be so scared. The next time you're scared, remember that God is with you.

1. What's the scariest thing you've ever done?
2. Who is a helper God has given you to help calm your fears?
3. When we're afraid, how can we remember that God is with us?

Dear God,
    Sometimes I get scared. I don't want to, but I do. Help me to trust you always. I know you're with me. Amen.

Being Stubborn
EXODUS 8

The Lord . . . caused the swarms to go away, so that not one remained. But Pharaoh hardened his heart again. He did not let the people go!

EXODUS 8:31-32

You can read more about the stubborn king of Egypt on page 90 of *The Eager Reader Bible*.

The king of Egypt kept the Hebrews as slaves. God said to him, "Let my people go!" But the stubborn king did not care about God's message. He would not do it. So God sent plagues to change the king's mind. The king STILL would not budge. Nine times God sent plagues. Nine times the king said no. In the end, the stubborn king lost the slaves and a whole lot more. Many people suffered because he wouldn't listen. Sometimes it's best to change your no to a yes.

1. What does it mean to be stubborn?
2. When was a time you thought someone was being stubborn?
3. How are other people hurt when someone is stubborn?

Dear God,
   Please forgive me when I am stubborn. Help me to do what I am told. Amen.

The Lord gave the Israelites favor with the Egyptians. They gave them whatever they wanted. The Egyptians were practically stripped of all they owned!

EXODUS 12:36

You can read more about God's people in Egypt on page 86 of *The Eager Reader Bible.*

God's people were slaves in Egypt. They wanted to be free more than anything. Moses and Aaron had asked the king of Egypt nine times to let them go. Nine times the king said, "NO!" But God changed the king's mind. And soon God's people got to go free! God's team is the best team. God is always working for us. Even when things look hopeless, don't give up on God!

1. What teams or groups are you part of?
2. What is the best thing about being on a team?
3. How can you keep from quitting God's team?

Dear God,
    Thank you for putting me on your team.
I will always cheer for your side! Amen.

**Moses told the people, "Don't be afraid.
Just stand where you are and watch. You
will see the wonderful way the Lord will
rescue you today."**

EXODUS 14:13

You can read more about Moses and God's people escaping
from the Egyptians on page 98 of *The Eager Reader Bible*.

God's people were escaping Egypt, but they were trapped by a great sea. The Egyptians were chasing them. God's people began to whine and cry, "Oh no! We never should have left Egypt. Now we're going to die! Ahhh!" Moses told the people to calm down. "God will save us," Moses said. "Don't be so upset!" Just then, the great sea opened up, and the people of God crossed over. God saved his people. They didn't need to whine at all! Believe in God's help instead of whining.

1. What do whiners sound like?
2. Why are whiners no fun to be around?
3. When you feel like whining, what is one thing you can do instead?

Dear Lord,
   You are mighty and awesome. When I feel like whining, please help me to say, "God will work it out" instead. Amen.

Sing to God!
EXODUS 15

Then Miriam the prophetess, the sister of Aaron, took a tambourine and led the women in dances. And Miriam sang this song: Sing to the Lord, for he has won gloriously!

EXODUS 15:20-21

You can read more about Miriam's song on page 102 of *The Eager Reader Bible*.

People make up songs about all sorts of things. Miriam made up a song when God rescued his people from the Egyptians. She wrote a song of praise. The song tells about how great God is. The song tells about the good things God did. The song praises God because he saved his people. Miriam's song made everyone happy. The people danced and laughed and clapped as they remembered how God had helped them!

1. How do you think God feels when we sing songs to him?
2. What has happened this week to remind you how great and good God is?
3. If you wrote a song to God, what would it say?

> *Dear God,*
>   *You are strong and good to all your people. Thank you for loving me. I love you, too!*
> *Amen.*

Eating
EXODUS 16

Moses told them, "Don't leave it overnight."

EXODUS 16:19

You can read about God sending food on
page 106 of *The Eager Reader Bible.*

Going on a hike with Mom and Dad can be fun. But if they hike too far, any kid will get grumpy. "Hey, Mom, when can we go back?" Or: "Hey, Dad, when can we eat?" After the Hebrew kids had walked all day, they too were hungry. There was no time to plant crops or hunt, so God sent food. It was called *manna*. God made sure they always had enough. They could have as much as they wanted—as long as they didn't waste it. That's a good rule for us today, too.

1. If you had to eat one kind of food all year, what would you want to eat?
2. What friend's house has great snacks lying around the kitchen, waiting for hungry kids to come over?
3. In what ways have you wasted food?

Dear God,
    Thank you for food. Help me not to waste it and to share it whenever I can. Amen.

Mom and Dad
Exodus 19:1—20:21

Honor your father and mother. Do this that you may have a long, good life in the land the Lord your God will give you.

EXODUS 20:12

You can read about the Ten Commandments on page 110 of *The Eager Reader Bible.*

God gave 10 rules to help us know how to live. But one rule is especially for kids: "Honor your father and mother." It is the only rule with a promise: "Then you may have a long, good life." Is that a trick? No way. Moms and dads know things that kids don't know. They see dangers that kids can't see. So respect your mom and dad. Listen to their words, and copy what they do. Other kids will wonder how you got to be so smart.

1. What's one thing you have learned from your mom or dad?
2. What are three things your parents ask you to do?
3. How can kids show respect to their parents?

Dear God,
   Thank you for my parents. Please help me to honor and respect them. Amen.

Respect God's Name
Exodus 20:7

You shall not use the name of the Lord your God irreverently. Nor shall you use it to swear. You will not escape punishment if you do.

EXODUS 20:7

Have you ever heard someone say *God* or *Jesus* as a swearword? They aren't really talking to God. They just want to use his name like a bad word. Or they just say it for fun. That's a bad idea. God rules the whole universe. He is holy and awesome. We should never use his name as a cheap and ugly swearword. When you say God's name, go ahead and talk to him. Use other words when you're angry or goofing around.

1. Why do you think some people say *God* or *Jesus* as a swearword?
2. What songs do you know that have God's name or Jesus' name in them?
3. How do you feel when someone uses God's name the wrong way?

> *Dear God,*
>   *I'm glad I can talk to you. Please help me to use your name the right way. Amen.*

Admit Your Mistakes
EXODUS 32

A person who refuses to admit his mistakes can never be successful. But if he admits and leaves them, he gets another chance.

PROVERBS 28:13

You can read more about Aaron's mistake on page 114 of *The Eager Reader Bible*.

Moses went up a mountain to talk with God by himself. While he was gone, Aaron helped God's people make a golden cow to worship, instead of worshiping God! Moses came down from the mountain, and Aaron lied. Aaron said, "I just threw some gold into the fire. Then this cow came out by itself!" Aaron made a big mistake by helping to make the golden cow. But lying to Moses about it made it even worse. Aaron should have been honest and said he was sorry.

1. What did Aaron do wrong?
2. What good things happen in your family when you admit you made a mistake?
3. What's the best thing to do when you goof up?

Dear God,
 Sometimes I don't do the right thing. Help me to admit it when I make a mistake. Amen.

Protection
NUMBERS 13—14

[Joshua and Caleb said,] "Oh, do not rebel against the Lord. When the Lord is with you, don't be afraid of people who might hurt you. Don't be afraid of the people of the land. For they are but bread for us to eat!"

NUMBERS 14:9

You can read more about Joshua and Caleb on page 118 of *The Eager Reader Bible*.

God promised to give his people a wonderful new land. The land was filled with delicious food. The land was ALSO filled with big and strong enemies. God's people got scared. They thought they were going to get hurt. Joshua and Caleb said not to worry. "We can enter this new land," they said. "God is with us. He won't let us get hurt." But the people were still scared. They didn't trust God to protect them. So God did not let them go into the new land. God can protect us against any danger.

1. What were God's people so afraid of if God was protecting them?
2. What makes you feel safe?
3. When you're scared, who can you ask to protect you?

Dear God,
  Thank you for being my protector. Please help me always to trust you when I'm afraid. Amen.

A wise person controls his temper. He knows that anger causes mistakes.

PROVERBS 14:29

You can read more about Balaam and his donkey on page 122 of *The Eager Reader Bible.*

Balaam was angry. Balaam's donkey wouldn't do what he wanted it to do. Balaam told his donkey to go, but it wouldn't. So he hit the poor animal with a stick! Then the donkey talked, and an angel scolded Balaam! Then Balaam felt silly. Hitting his donkey didn't help anything. Losing his temper only made things worse. If you feel angry, go ahead and say how you feel. But don't lose your temper and hit things. Temper tantrums make you do silly things!

1. What barnyard animal would you like to be for a day? Why?
2. What do you feel like doing when you get really mad?
3. What are right ways and wrong ways to express angry feelings?

Dear God,
Help me to control my temper. When I feel angry, help me to talk about it but not to hit. Amen.

Ask Before You Take
DEUTERONOMY 5:19

You must not steal.

DEUTERONOMY 5:19

Taking something that doesn't belong to you is called *stealing*. Stealing is wrong, even if we take something small. It's wrong, even if we never get caught doing it. It's wrong, even if all our friends do it. God sees, and God remembers. Respect other people's things. If you want to borrow something, ask first. Otherwise it's stealing. And always be sure to bring it back when you're done.

1. How do you feel when someone borrows your things without asking?

2. What is something you don't have   but wish you did have?

3. What would happen if everyone in your family always asked before borrowing?

Dear God,
    Please help me to remember to ask before I take things. Amen.

Choosing Sides
JOSHUA 2

[Rahab said,] "No wonder we are afraid of you!
No one has any fight left after hearing things
like that! For your God is the supreme God of
heaven. He is not just an ordinary god."

JOSHUA 2:11

You can read more about Rahab helping Joshua's
spies on page 126 of *The Eager Reader Bible*.

Rahab had to make a tough decision. She could help Joshua's spies, or she could help the city police catch them. Who should she help? Joshua's spies were on God's side. Rahab knew it was better to be on God's side. So she helped them hide.

1. What do you think is neat about what Rahab did?
2. When do you have to choose sides? (Hint: Think of the games you play.)
3. What does it mean to be on God's side?

Dear God,
    Thank you for letting me be on your side. Please teach me to help your people the way Rahab did. Amen.

Include Your Friends
JOSHUA 6

Joshua saved Rahab. He also saved her relatives who were with her in the house. They still live among the Israelites because she hid the spies sent to Jericho by Joshua.

JOSHUA 6:25

You can read more about the rescue of Rahab and her family on page 130 of *The Eager Reader Bible*.

Joshua's men were spying in Jericho. Rahab kept the men safe from Jericho's evil king. Joshua did not forget about her kindness. Soon, God helped Joshua's people capture Jericho. But Joshua rescued Rahab and her family. Rahab was not one of God's people. But Joshua let her join them. He let her and her family be a part of their group. Joshua was a true friend to Rahab. He let her join his group.

1. How do you feel when you are left out of a group?

2. In what way did Joshua include Rahab?

3. What can you do to include other friends in your activities?

Dear God,
    Please show me how to include others. I want to be a true friend like Joshua was to Rahab. Amen.

The Lord turned to [Gideon]. He said, "I will make you strong! Go and save Israel from the Midianites! I am sending you!"

JUDGES 6:14

You can read more about Gideon on page 134 of *The Eager Reader Bible.*

Gideon felt small and helpless. His family was poor. His army had only a handful of men. And their weapons were not very good. But God gave him an important job. Gideon led his tiny army to win a great battle! God's angel said, "It doesn't matter if you feel small. You have a big and powerful God. He will help you." So Gideon relied on God. And God helped him. God can help you, too. When you feel small, rely on God.

1. When do you feel small or weak?
2. What makes you feel strong?
3. What do you think about the way Gideon trusted God?

Dear God,
   Thank you for helping small people. I will let you help me, too, instead of always trying to do it myself. Amen.

Keeping Secrets
JUDGES 16:1-22

She nagged at him every day until he couldn't stand it any longer. In the end, he told her his secret.

JUDGES 16:16-17

You can read more about mighty Samson on page 138 of *The Eager Reader Bible.*

A woman named Delilah begged Samson to tell her the secret of his strength. At first, Samson said no. He had promised God that he wouldn't tell. But Delilah kept begging. Finally, Samson broke his promise to God. Samson told Delilah his very special secret. Samson wasn't supposed to tell. Sometimes people try to cover up bad things and keep them secret. Bad secrets should NOT be secrets. If someone tells you about someone getting hurt, go ahead and tell. But if someone tells you a GOOD secret, be sure you keep it.

1. How do you feel when someone tells your secrets?
2. What is one kind of BAD secret you should tell an adult about?
3. How come GOOD secrets are never supposed to be told?

Dear God,
Help me to know the difference between good secrets I need to keep secret, and bad secrets I need to tell someone about. Amen.

A Story about Loyalty
RUTH 1—4

A true friend is always loyal. And a brother is born to help in time of need.

PROVERBS 17:17

You can read more about kind Ruth on page 142 of *The Eager Reader Bible.*

Naomi was old, lonely, and sad. Her husband and two sons had died. She was very far from her home in Israel. She didn't want to go back to Israel all by herself. So Ruth said, "Don't worry. I'll go with you." Ruth went to Israel with Naomi. She worked and worked so Naomi could have food. Then Ruth got married to a man named Boaz, and Naomi came to live with them. Naomi wasn't alone because she had Ruth. Ruth was a true and loyal friend—the best kind anybody can be.

1. What was so neat about what Ruth did?
2. When was a time you felt scared and all alone?
3. What are some ways a kid can be a loyal friend?

Dear God,
 Thank you for my friends and family. Help me to be true and loyal to them all. Amen.

Answered Prayer
1 SAMUEL 1:1—2:11

This was Hannah's prayer: "How I rejoice in the Lord! How he has blessed me! Now I have an answer for my enemies, for the Lord has solved my problem. How I rejoice!"

1 SAMUEL 2:1

You can read more about Hannah's prayer on page 146 of *The Eager Reader Bible*.

Kids sometimes dream about one special thing they want most of all. So do adults. Hannah dreamed about her one special wish: to have a baby. So she prayed. And God granted her request. He gave her a baby boy, and she named the baby Samuel. What did Hannah do when her dream came true? She told God how happy she was. She even sang a song of praise to God. Hannah let everyone know that God had given her a precious, special, awesome, really big wish. Let people know when God answers your prayers!

1. What special wishes do you have?
2. Who knows what your special wishes are?
3. How can you thank God for answering your prayers?

Dear God,
My special, really big wish is _____.
When it comes, I'll be very, very grateful.
Amen.

I Want One, Too!
1 SAMUEL 8

"Give us a king like all the other nations have," they pleaded.

1 SAMUEL 8:5

You can read more about Israel's first king on page 150 of *The Eager Reader Bible.*

God's people were unhappy. They did not have a king. God was their king. But they were jealous of the other nations. All the other nations had human kings. "If only we had a king," God's people moaned. "THEN we would be happy!" Samuel told them they would be sorry if they got a king. And Samuel was right. Their kings brought them a LOT of trouble. They learned that it's better to be happy with God's plan for us than to want what other people have.

1. When have you been jealous of what someone else has?
2. What do you think God's people should have done when Samuel said they didn't need a king?
3. When do you need to remember to be content?

Dear God,
   I am glad for all you have given me. Please teach me to be content with what I have.
Amen.

Obedience
1 SAMUEL 15:1-23

"What pleases the Lord the most? . . . It is much better to obey the Lord than to give him an offering. It is much better to listen to him than to offer him something."

1 SAMUEL 15:22

You can read more about David and Saul on page 154 of *The Eager Reader Bible.*

Saul was the first king of God's people. But he did not obey God very much. *I'm a great king!* he thought to himself. *I don't have to obey God.* But God wanted a king who would obey him. So he told his messenger Samuel to make David the next king. David loved God and obeyed him. God likes it when we give things to him. But he likes it even more when we obey him.

1. What was the difference between Saul and David?
2. What are God's rules for us today?
3. Who do you know who really tries to obey God?

Dear God,
You are in charge of my life. Please teach me to obey you all the time. Amen.

**The Lord said to Samuel, ". . . People accept
others by the way they look on the outside.
But I look inside a person. I look at a
person's heart and thoughts."**

1 SAMUEL 16:7

Israel needed a new king, and Saul's son Eliab was strong and handsome. Samuel thought Eliab would make a good king. But God said no. Being tall and handsome is not what counts with God. God wants leaders who tell the truth, do what is right, and protect everyone. God cares most about the way you behave, not whether you are handsome or pretty. Be the kind of person that God would want for a leader.

1. Why do kids want to look handsome or pretty?
2. Why do leaders need to be honest and good more than handsome or pretty?
3. What's one thing your mom or dad can do to help you be honest and good?

> *Dear God,*
>   *I want to be honest, good, and strong because that's the best kind of leader. Amen.*

Courage
1 SAMUEL 17

David shouted in reply, "You come to me with a sword and spear. But I come to you in the name of the Lord of the armies of heaven and of Israel."

1 SAMUEL 17:45

You can read more about David and Goliath on page 158 of *The Eager Reader Bible.*

Goliath hated God's people. Goliath scared EVERYBODY. But David was not afraid of Goliath. David knew that God was way bigger than Goliath. God could do ANYTHING, and God would help him. David was small, and Goliath was big. David was kind, and Goliath was mean. But David knew that God was on his side. He loved God and wanted to defend God's people. That's how God made David brave. That's how you can be brave, too.

1. Who do you think is the bravest person in the world? Why?
2. When do you think it's hard to be brave?
3. What do you think is neat about what David did?

Dear God,
  Thank you for being strong and mighty. Please help me be a brave person. Amen.

Don't Be Jealous
1 SAMUEL 18:1—19:18

Saul was afraid of David. He was jealous because the Lord had left him and was now with David.

1 SAMUEL 18:12

David was a brave fighter and a great friend. Just about everybody liked David. But King Saul did not like him. Saul felt jealous of David. He thought David got way too much attention. So he tried to hurt David. David wanted to be Saul's friend. But Saul would not let him, simply because Saul was jealous. He chased David away and lost a great helper and friend. Be glad instead of jealous when your friends do well.

1. What does it mean to be jealous?
2. How do you think David felt when Saul threw a spear at him?
3. What do you need to do if you feel jealous of a friend?

Dear God,
    Thank you for my friends. Help me to be glad and not jealous when they do well. Amen.

How to Deal with Mean People
1 SAMUEL 24

**[King Saul] said to David, "You are a
better man than I am. You have repaid
me good for evil."**

1 SAMUEL 24:17

You can read more about David's kindness to
Saul on page 166 of *The Eager Reader Bible.*

Normally if a kid calls you a name, you want to call him names, too. If a kid tries to trip you or push you, you want to push back. But God showed David a better way. Saul was trying to hurt David. One day David had Saul right where he wanted him, alone in a cave. But instead of hurting him, David let him go. David was kind to Saul because God was in David's heart. Be nice to mean people instead of being mean back.

1. What do you do if a kid kicks or hits you?
2. Why is God pleased when we are kind?
3. What should you do if kids laugh at you for being kind?

Dear God,
Help me to be kind to bullies. It's not easy, but I'll try with your help. Amen.

Dear friends, if people are mean to you,
don't try to get even. Leave that to God. He
has said that he will pay them back.

ROMANS 12:19

Saul had tried to hurt David. Now David had a chance to hurt Saul. Saul was asleep in his tent. David and his friend sneaked up on him. David's friend whispered, "Here is your chance to hurt Saul!" But David did nothing. He knew that someday God would punish Saul. If David hurt Saul, it would only bring David new problems. So David left Saul alone. David let God take care of punishing Saul.

1. What did David do instead of getting back at Saul?
2. When was a time you wanted to get back at somebody for hurting you?
3. What can you do the next time you want to get back at somebody for hurting you?

Dear God,
*   I want to be like David. Help me not to get back at people but to let you deal with them. Amen.*

Leaders of all the tribes of Israel now came to David at Hebron. There they promised him that they would be loyal.

2 SAMUEL 5:1

You can read more about David becoming king on page 170 of *The Eager Reader Bible*.

God chose David to be the second king of Israel. But some people did not like God's choice. They wanted Saul's son Ish-bosheth to be king. Ish-bosheth did not follow God as David did. Ish-bosheth and his leaders fought against David. But David won. David was crowned the one and only king. And the people of Israel then promised always to follow David. Help God's leaders—don't fight against them.

1. What was wrong with choosing another king besides David?
2. Who are your leaders at home? at school? at church?
3. What can you do to be a helper for your leaders?

Dear God,
   Thank you for my leaders. Please show me how to be loyal to them. Amen.

Stealing
1 KINGS 3:16-28

You must not steal.

EXODUS 20:15

You can read more about Solomon and the two women on page 174 of *The Eager Reader Bible*.

One day two women came to see King Solomon. They both wanted the same baby. Both women said, "I am the baby's mother." Solomon found out who was the real mother and gave the baby to her. The other woman had tried to steal the baby. God does not want us to steal anything. "You must not steal" is one of his most important rules. Never take what belongs to someone else!

1. Why do you think people steal from each other?
2. Have you ever had anything stolen from you?
3. How can you and your family make "Do not steal" one of your most important rules?

Dear God,
    Thank you for giving me all I need.
Please help me never to steal other people's things. Amen.

God Is Great!
1 KINGS 8

Solomon . . . said, "O Lord God of Israel! There is no god like you in heaven or earth! You are loving and kind. You keep your promises to your people if they do their best to do your will."

1 KINGS 8:22-23

You can read more about God's great Temple on page 178 of *The Eager Reader Bible.*

God's Temple was finally finished. Solomon, the king of Israel, stood in front of all God's people and praised God. Solomon showed his love for God by praising him. The people of God finally had a place to worship God. The Temple was beautiful. Inside, the people sang praises to God. They danced. They laughed. They prayed. Solomon led all the people in praising God. God deserves our praise!

1. What is the thing you like best about God?
2. What are different ways to praise the Lord?
3. What do you want to praise God for today?

Dear God,
I praise you for blessing me every day. I praise you for your kindness and gentleness to me. Amen.

Tell Others about God
1 KINGS 18:1-40

Elijah talked to them. "How long will you try to serve both Baal and the Lord?" he asked the people. "If the Lord is God, *follow* him!"

1 KINGS 18:21

Elijah's neighbors were mixed up. Instead of believing in the God of the Bible, they made up their own gods. Instead of serving the one true God, they served pretend gods. Elijah could have kept quiet about it. But Elijah was bold. He talked about the Lord. Then he asked God to show the people the truth. And God did. Because Elijah was bold, the people of Israel found out that the Lord really is the one true God. Be bold like Elijah.

1. Who is the boldest person you know?
2. What are some ways God shows people that he is real?
3. Which of your friends would you like to tell about the one true God?

Dear God,
    Please give me the boldness to tell one of my friends about you today. Amen.

Teasing
2 Kings 2:23-25

As [Elisha] was walking along the road, a gang of young men began making fun of him. They had come from the city. They made fun of him because his head was bald. He turned around and cursed them in the name of the Lord. Suddenly two female bears came out of the woods. The bears tore up 42 of them.

2 KINGS 2:23-24

It's fun to kid around with others. But sometimes we go too far. We tease people. We make fun of them. We call them names. We make them feel stupid or ugly. God doesn't like it when we do that. He wants us to respect others, not make fun of them. Do you know somebody who is different? Respect that person. Say nice things or say nothing. Do not tease or make fun of anyone.

1. What kid do you know who gets teased a lot?
2. What is something respectful you could tell a friend or family member today?
3. What would your friends say if you made it a rule never to tease people in your games?

Dear God,
Help me to respect others and not to tease them. Amen.

Protect Little Kids
2 CHRONICLES 22:9—23:11

They brought out the little prince. They put
the crown on his head. . . . A great shout
went up. "Long live the king!" they said.

2 CHRONICLES 23:11

You can read more about how the boy Joash became
king on page 186 of *The Eager Reader Bible*.

How did Joash get to be king? It was because of his aunt and uncle. Prince Joash's evil grandmother wanted to kill him so that she could be queen. But Joash's aunt and uncle put him in a secret room. Then when Joash turned seven, they brought him out and crowned him king. Joash was safe, and his evil grandmother's plans were spoiled. Joash's aunt and uncle protected a little kid who could not protect himself. We should protect little kids from bullies and danger.

1. Who protects you from bullies and danger?
2. How can you be a protector of little kids?
3. When bad or evil people want to hurt you, what can you do?

Dear God,
*   I want to be a defender of little kids, just like Joash's aunt and uncle. Please make me brave when I need to be. Amen.*

Don't Listen to Troublemakers
EZRA 4—6

The Lord was taking care of this problem. So our enemies did not make us stop building.

EZRA 5:5

You can read more about the new Temple on page 222 of *The Eager Reader Bible.*

One minute God's people were happy. They were rebuilding God's Temple. But then some troublemakers came and started acting tough. They made up stories and lied to the king. They said to God's people, "We're going to hurt you!" God sent prophets to the rescue. "I will watch over you," God said. "Don't be afraid. Keep on working!" So the people thought about God, instead of the troublemakers, and finished the work. Don't listen to troublemakers—believe what God says!

1. What is a troublemaker?
2. How can we keep troublemakers from making us scared?
3. If you were to build a new church building, what would it look like?

Dear God,
I want to serve you. Help me not to listen to troublemakers who try to make me stop. Amen.

Help Someone Finish
NEHEMIAH 4

**[Nehemiah said,] "Don't be afraid!
. . . Remember the Lord. He is
great and strong!"**

NEHEMIAH 4:14

You can read more about Nehemiah on
page 226 of *The Eager Reader Bible*.

The city of Jerusalem needed walls for protection. But the workers were sad. They had lots of problems. Their enemies got them in trouble with the king. Nehemiah knew what the workers needed. "Never mind that our enemies are laughing," he said. "Never mind that we don't have enough supplies. Never mind that your muscles are tired. God is great, and he will help us!" The workers listened. They went back to work. And God did help them. And they finished the wall. Nehemiah was right. Be a finisher.

1. Around your house, what big project do you wish would get done?
2. How can God help you today to finish an important job?
3. What can you do to encourage a worker who feels like giving up?

Dear God,
    Please help me always to finish my chores, so someday, when I'm big, I'll know how to be a finisher. Amen.

Brave Queen Esther
Esther 3—7

I have followed your commands. I have not gone along with cruel and evil men.

PSALM 17:4

You can read more about brave Queen Esther on page 218 of *The Eager Reader Bible*.

Haman hated Mordecai. Mordecai was Jewish and so was his cousin, Queen Esther. Haman could think of only one thing: hurting Mordecai. So he hatched a plot to have Mordecai killed, and all the other Jews, too. But Mordecai discovered Haman's plot. He got Queen Esther to help. Soon the king knew all about Haman's evil plot. And the king had him put to death. Haman was an evil man. He tried to hurt innocent people. That's something that God's people must never do.

1. How did Queen Esther and Mordecai save all the Jews?
2. Why is it sometimes hard to be brave against someone who talks tough?
3. How can you be a protector like Esther and Mordecai were?

> *Dear God,*
> *Please help me never to hurt anyone. And please teach me to be a protector like Mordecai and Queen Esther. Amen.*

Conscience
JOB 27

Cling tightly to your faith in Christ. Always keep your conscience clear, doing what you know is right. Some people have not obeyed their consciences. They know they have done what was wrong.

1 TIMOTHY 1:19

Everything was going wrong for Job. Some people said, "God is punishing you for your sin. Don't you feel guilty?" But Job did not feel guilty because he had done nothing wrong. He tried hard to do what was right. So when people said that he had done wrong, he did not have to feel bad. You know what is right. Be sure to do it! Then your conscience will be clear. Then you will not feel guilty.

1. Why was Job able to say, "I don't feel guilty"?
2. What are some things that you know in your heart are bad to do?
3. What are some things that you know in your heart are good to do?

Dear God,
    Thank you for my conscience. Help me do what I know to be right. Help me not to sin when I know better. Amen.

Bad-mouthing
Psalm 15:3

He doesn't lie about others. He never listens
to gossip. He doesn't harm his neighbor.

PSALM 15:3

It's easy to bad-mouth some other kid when he's not around. You can make fun of him, laugh about him, tell the secrets he tells you, and he doesn't even know it. When you start talking about someone, make sure you brag about her. Don't just criticize or laugh at her. Then when you meet the person again, you won't have to worry about what you have said. Good playmates don't bad-mouth each other.

1. What kinds of things do you want people to say about you when you're not around?
2. When is it OK to talk about others?
3. How do you know when you should stop talking about someone else?

Dear God,
   Sometimes my words hurt other people. Help me always to speak well of others when they aren't around to hear me say it. Amen.

Memorize a Bible Verse
Psalm 19:7-8

God's laws are perfect. They protect us and make us wise. They give us joy and light.

PSALM 19:7-8

Think of all the things boys and girls can memorize: where they live, their birthday, their phone number, or the letters of the alphabet. Maybe you know some of these things by heart. It helps when we store facts like these in our mind. Then we always have them with us. That's why it helps to memorize verses from the Bible. It makes us always have God's Word with us. Wherever we go, we know how God wants us to live!

1. What are some of the things you have memorized?
2. What kinds of things do you like to remember most?
3. What Bible verses have you memorized?

Dear God,
Thank you for the Bible. It is a great treasure. Help me to memorize a verse this week. Amen.

[The Lord's king] feels pity for the weak and needy. And he will rescue them.

PSALM 72:13

I'm big and strong," said a kid. But he never acted like it. When a kid at the mall started crying because he was lost, the "big kid" just laughed. When one of his friends started pushing around a kindergarten kid and making her cry, the "big kid" just watched. A kid who brags about being big, but never helps kids who are in   trouble, isn't so big after all. God wants us to help people in trouble whenever we can.

1. What older kid (or bigger kid) has helped you a lot?
2. What's wrong with ignoring people who need help?
3. When is it good to ask adults for help instead of doing it yourself?

Dear God,
Help me always to be ready and brave to help people in trouble. Amen.

I will make the godly of the land my heroes.
I will invite them to my home. Only those
who are truly good shall be my servants.

PSALM 101:6

132

This psalm writer wanted a special kind of
hero. He wanted a hero who loved God. He didn't
want just any kind of hero. Everybody has a hero.
Sometimes our heroes come from stories, or sports,
or TV. The best heroes love God with all their heart
and follow God with all their energy. They give
credit to God for all they get done. They pray to
God and trust God. Heroes like that make people
want to be great—and to be great for the right
reasons and in the right way. Have a hero like that.

1. Who do you really want to be like when you
   grow up?
2. Who would make a really good hero?
3. What books around your house
   tell stories of great heroes? (Ask
   Mom or Dad to read one to you
   instead of watching TV tonight.)

Dear God,
    I want to follow great heroes. Help Mom
and Dad and me to read and learn about
them so that I can be like them. Amen.

Sing a Praise Song to God
PSALM 147:1

Praise the Lord! Yes, praise the Lord! How good it is to sing his praises! How delightful, and how right!

PSALM 147:1

134

Do you listen to the radio? Every day people from all over the world listen to songs on the radio. Happy songs. Sad songs. Funny songs. Songs that make you smile. The Bible says to sing songs to God. Songs that praise God for his love and kindness. Songs that make God smile. Songs that tell of God's joy and peace. Every day you can sing songs of praise to God.

1. What is your favorite song?
2. What Bible songs do you know? (See how long a list you can make.)
3. How do you think God feels when we sing to him?

Dear Lord,
   I think it's neat that you like to hear us praise you. No one deserves more praise than you! Amen.

Rebels
PROVERBS 1:10, 15-16

Sinners might say to you, "Come and join us." But if they do, turn your back on them! . . . Stay far from people like that!

PROVERBS 1:10, 15

Some kids like to break rules. They think they're tough. They think it's cool to disobey. If you're smart, you'll stay away from them. They will get into big trouble. If you follow them, you'll get into trouble, too. That will make Mom and Dad really sad, not to mention how sad YOU'LL be. Wise kids don't make friends with rebels. They know when to say, "Forget it, I'm not doing that. It's wrong!"

1. How have you seen kids get into trouble by breaking the rules?
2. Why do you think the Bible tells us to stay away from kids who like to break the rules?
3. Who would be sad if you got into big trouble?

Dear God,
    I want Mom and Dad to be happy with me. Help me obey the rules and say no when other kids invite me to be a rebel. Amen.

Real Treasure
PROVERBS 2:6

The Lord gives wisdom! His every word is a treasure of knowledge.

PROVERBS 2:6

Have you ever been on a treasure hunt? It's really fun, isn't it? And what a treat when you find the treasure and get to keep it! God's Word is a treasure chest. Inside you can find all kinds of treasure. There's so much that it takes a whole lifetime to dig it all out! Read the Bible—by yourself and with your family. Go to church to learn even more. Then you will find some REAL treasure!

1. What would you like to learn about God?
2. What kind of treasure have you found in the Bible?
3. Who can help you find some more treasure in the Bible?

Dear God,
   I want to find some of your treasure. Teach me what I need to know from the Bible. Amen.

Plans
PROVERBS 3:29

Don't make evil plans against your neighbor. He is trusting you.

PROVERBS 3:29

Builders make floor plans. Kids plan sleep-overs. Families make dinner plans. But no one should ever make a plan to hurt people. Some kids plan bad jokes to play on other kids. Some make plans to tell a lie about other kids to get them into trouble. But these plans hurt people, like Joseph's brothers' plans hurt him. Instead, make a plan to be extra nice one day. Or plan to play with friends. A good plan always helps someone.

1. When did you and your friend plan a fun time together?
2. How could you plan something nice for your family?
3. What could you plan to do with friends this week?

Dear God,
   Thank you for friends and family. Teach me to make plans to help and not harm them. Amen.

Mom and Dad
PROVERBS 6:20-21

Young person, obey your father and your mother. Take to heart all of their advice. Keep in mind all that they tell you.

PROVERBS 6:20-21

Did you ever wonder what to do? Did you ever wish you knew more stuff? Did you ever hear a lie and need to know the truth? Did you ever want to learn something hard? Did you ever need to find answers? That's why God gave you a mom and a dad. They may not always be around. They may not always make you happy. But they have wisdom that's just for you.

1. What is one thing your mom or dad has taught you?
2. What do you most want to learn from your mom or dad?
3. If you have only one parent, who can you ask to teach you mom-stuff or dad-stuff?

Dear God,
Thank you for my parents. Help me to learn from them a little bit each day. Amen.

Hatred stirs old quarrels. But love overlooks insults.

PROVERBS 10:12

Have you ever heard someone say, "I hate you?" I hope not. Hate causes all sorts of problems. Hate makes people sad. Hate makes people fight. Hate makes people cry. Hate does nobody any good. God tells us to love people instead of hate people. Give hugs instead of hits. Say "I love you" instead of "I hate you." Call people neat instead of names. That makes God happy.

1. What is the best thing you could ever say to someone? (Hint: Think up your favorite.)
2. What kinds of things can you do instead of hating someone?
3. What would your neighborhood be like if everyone hated each other?

Dear God,
*   Thank you for always loving me. Help me never to hate anyone. Amen.*

Don't Have Fun Being Bad
PROVERBS 10:23

A fool has fun by being bad. A wise person has fun by being wise!

PROVERBS 10:23

Do you like to have fun? Everyone likes to laugh. There's nothing better than being with friends and feeling happy. But watch out! Some boys and girls have fun doing bad things. They go places they know they shouldn't go. They say things they know are wrong. They invite their friends to do the same. It may be fun to do something bad, but it isn't very smart.

1. What is the most fun activity you have ever done?
2. What kinds of things arc not fun for you?
3. What is something fun you would like to do with your family?

Dear God,
   I'm glad you want us to be happy. Please teach me to have fun in ways that honor you. Amen.

Don't Fight
PROVERBS 11:12

To argue with a neighbor is foolish. A
person with good sense holds his tongue.

PROVERBS 11:12

It's easy to get into fights. If someone takes your stuff or bothers you, you may want to fight. But "to argue with a neighbor is foolish. A person with good sense holds his tongue." So cool down! Talk it out! Keep your friends!

1. Why do people argue?
2. What do you and your friends argue about?
3. What do you want to remember next time you feel like punching somebody?

Dear God,
I know that you really hate fighting. Please help me to hate it just as much as you do. Amen.

Learn from Mistakes
PROVERBS 12:1

To learn you must want to be taught. To refuse teaching is stupid.

PROVERBS 12:1

A football star. A tennis pro. A champion runner. What do these people have in common? They each learn from a good coach. The coaches correct their mistakes. The coaches want them to learn the best way to play. The players who want to get better listen to their coaches. Parents and teachers can be your coaches. Don't feel too bad when they want you to do better. Just learn what you can and try again!

1. What do you like to learn about?
2. Who are your favorite teachers?
3. What good lesson have you
   learned from a yucky mistake?

Dear God,
  Thank you for people who teach me. Please help me to learn from my mistakes. Amen.

Join Somebody in Something Good
PROVERBS 12:2

The Lord blesses good people and condemns the wicked.

PROVERBS 12:2

Instead of doing good things, some kids plan to do bad things. Mean tricks. Lying. Stealing. Making fun of other kids. Doing bad things only hurts people. Bad things spoil our fun. Here's a great idea: Why don't you get some friends and plan something good? Plan fun things to do. Do something good for someone else. Take out the trash. Sing a special song. Help clean the house. Do something good today!

1. What is something good someone has done for you?
2. Who can you get together with to do something good?
3. Who can you do something good for today?

Dear God,
    Please help me to do something good today. Show me someone you want me to make happy. Amen.

Take Care of Your Pet
PROVERBS 12:10

A good person is concerned for the welfare
of his animals. But even the kindness of
godless people is cruel.

PROVERBS 12:10

If you have a pet, whose chore is it to take care of it? to walk your family's dog? to clean up the kitty litter? or to feed the guinea pigs? Lots of kids love pets. But sometimes kids don't love the work of keeping them clean and healthy. Some kids think it's yucky to clean up after their animals. Or they think it's icky to wash a pet or pick out fleas. But God wants us to take care of our animals. Be sure to show your pets some love and care today.

1. What pet chores can kids do best?
2. If you could have another pet, what would it be? Why?
3. What makes God happy about your care of pets?

Dear God,
*   I love _____ (your pet's name). Help me to take care of my pet and do the icky parts as well as the fun parts. Amen.*

Don't Lose Your Temper
PROVERBS 12:16

A fool is quick-tempered. A wise person stays cool when he is insulted.

PROVERBS 12:16

Have you ever seen or heard a firecracker go off? It has a very short fuse. Soon after it is lit with a match—*bang!* Get out of the way and cover your ears! Some people are like that. They get angry quickly and easily. When somebody says something they don't like, they make a big bang. Nobody enjoys being around a firecracker person. Try to stay calm when you start to get angry. If you do, you will enjoy life more and have more friends.

1. How do you feel around kids who lose their temper a lot?
2. Which of your friends keeps cool the best? How?
3. What things make it hard for you to keep your cool?

Dear God,
  Please help me not to blow up when things don't go my way. Show me how to stay calm. Amen.

Say You're Sorry
PROVERBS 15:1

A gentle answer turns away anger. But harsh words cause fights.

PROVERBS 15:1

Now say you're sorry!" How many times do you think you've heard that from parents or teachers? About a million? You may be sick of it, but it's still a good idea. When you hurt someone by hitting or with words, stop a moment. Think about how you would feel if you were hurt. Tell the person you are sorry. It is important to God and to the other person. Make it important to you.

1. How do you feel when someone hurts you and does not say sorry?
2. How does it help to say "I'm sorry" after you hurt someone?
3. When is it hard to say you're sorry?

Dear God,
  Hitting and name-calling can really hurt. Help me to say I'm sorry when I forget and hurt others. Amen.

A Verse about Being Fair
Proverbs 16:11

**The Lord demands fairness in every
business deal. He made this rule.**

PROVERBS 16:11

"THAT'S NOT FAIR!" Have you ever said that? Most boys and girls have. We say those words when someone cheats us. We say those words when someone breaks a promise. We say those words when someone changes the rules in the middle of a game. We say those words when others won't let us explain. No one likes to be treated unfairly. That's why God wants us to be fair. He is always fair with us, so we should be fair with each other.

1. Who is the fairest person you know?
2. What rules do you think are unfair? Why?
3. What is the fairest way to decide who gets to go first in a game?

Dear God,
I am glad you are perfectly fair. Help me to be fair all the time. Amen.

Be Polite
PROVERBS 16:24

Kind words are like honey. They are nice to hear and they bring health.

PROVERBS 16:24

Kindness is like a magnet. It will draw friends to the person who is kind. People like to be around someone who is kind. That kind someone could be you! Kindness is the key to making good friends. Try to be kind each day. Be polite when you talk. A kind word means a lot to people. Soon you will see how much people like to have you around!

1. Which of your friends is especially kind?
2. Why doesn't a rude person have many friends?
3. How can you be polite to your friends?

Dear God,
   Show me how to be kind. Please help me to be polite with others. Amen.

A Verse about Gossip
Proverbs 16:28

An evil person plants trouble. Gossip pulls the best of friends apart.

PROVERBS 16:28

Some boys and girls say mean things about other people. They whisper a lot. They share secrets (after they promised not to tell!). They talk about other boys and girls in unkind ways. That's gossip. Gossip makes God sad. And gossip makes friends stop being friends. A good friend tries to say good things about people, not mean things. A good friend doesn't whisper bad secrets about friends.

1. Why is it fun to say things about other people?
2. When is it OK to talk about others, and when is it NOT OK?
3. What kinds of things can we say about people instead of gossip?

Dear God,
    I don't want to cause trouble for others. Please help me not to gossip about people. Amen.

Don't Make Fun of Kids
PROVERBS 17:5

Laughing at the poor is like laughing at the
God who made them. He will punish those
who rejoice at others' troubles.

PROVERBS 17:5

Not far from where you live there's a kid who can't do what you can do. Maybe he has a bad sickness. Or maybe she can't walk. Or maybe their whole family has very little money. Some kids just don't have much. God cares a lot about those kids. They have a really tough time doing stuff, and that makes God sad. Don't make fun of kids who have less than you. Instead, be their friend. GOD is.

1. What's wrong with making fun of nerds, ugly kids, slow runners, or kids who have raggedy clothes?

2. What does God think when kids make fun of someone who's sick, hurt, or poor?
3. What do you think kids might make fun of you about?

> *Dear God,*
> *   Making fun of kids hurts them. Change my heart so that I will want to help kids, be their friend, and stick up for them. Amen.*

Be a Good Sport
PROVERBS 18:19

It is hard to win back the friendship of an offended brother. It is harder than capturing a city with great walls around it. His anger shuts you out like iron bars.

PROVERBS 18:19

Sometimes you win, sometimes you lose. Nobody wins every time. If you pout and cry when you lose, other kids won't want to play with you. If a friend beats you in a race, say, "You ran a good race!" If a kid from another school beats you in a spelling bee, say, "You're a good speller!" If your brother wins at a game you play together, say, "Nice job! Let's play again sometime." Instead of feeling crummy, praise the winner.

1. What's hard about being a good sport?
2. How can you be a good sport even when you win?
3. What can you learn from losing that you cannot learn from winning all the time?

> *Dear God,*
>   *When I lose a game, teach me not to pout. When I win, help me not to brag. Amen.*

Keep Your Cool
PROVERBS 19:11

A wise person holds back his anger and
overlooks insults. This is to his credit.

PROVERBS 19:11

Do you get angry when kids call you names? Or how about when kids laugh at you? It's easy to get angry and yell when you're picked on. But guess what? Bullies and mean kids WANT you to get angry. The best way to make them stop is just to walk away. Plug your ears, or start to sing. Keep your cool, and you will win. Don't get mad, and they will lose.

1. Why do you think some kids pick on others?
2. What kind of name-calling or teasing makes you angry?
3. What do you want to remember the next time a kid tries to make you mad?

Dear God,
   Help me to control my anger when kids pick on me. Help me just to ignore them. Amen.

Helping Needy People
PROVERBS 19:17

When you help the poor you are lending
to the Lord. He pays wonderful interest
on your loan!

PROVERBS 19:17

Everyone is special to God. But some people are extra special. They are not movie stars. They are poor people. They are people who do not have enough money, food, or clothes. They need God's help and yours. God can use you to show them his love. How can you help them? When someone needs some lunch money, you can give him some of yours. When someone wants a toy, you can share one of yours. You can always share what you have!

1. When was a time you shared something with a person who had nothing?
2. What do you think is neat about helping people?
3. How could your family join together to help a friend or neighbor?

Dear God,
Help me care for poor people. Teach me how to show them your love. Amen.

Keep Your Promises
PROVERBS 20:25

It is foolish to make a promise to the Lord before counting the cost.

PROVERBS 20:25

Have you ever broken a toy? It probably made you very sad. The same thing happens when people break their promises. Broken toys and broken promises are no fun. God says never to make a promise you can't keep. When you make a promise to someone, the other person counts on you to keep it. What happens if you don't keep your promise? The other person becomes sad and doesn't want to believe you anymore. Make promises only if you can keep them.

1. What kinds of promises do kids make to each other?
2. Why are promises so important?
3. What happens when people keep their promises?

Dear God,
    Please help me to make promises I can keep. Thank you for helping me keep my promises. Amen.

Saving a Little
PROVERBS 21:20

The wise person saves for the future. But the foolish person spends whatever he gets.

PROVERBS 21:20

Go into any store and you will find plenty of ways to spend your money. Some are nice treats once in a while. But always spending whatever is in your pocket to buy stuff will make you poor and sorry. If you save your money, you will have enough to buy something really special sometime. That is a good feeling. It also means you will have money to help others.

1. What things would you like to save up for?
2. How could you save up for some of the things you want?
3. Why do you think it is wise to save for the future?

Dear God,
    Thank you for trusting me with money.
Help me not to spend it all on junk. Amen.

Make a New Friend
PROVERBS 22:11

He who values grace and truth is the king's friend.

PROVERBS 22:11

Imagine being in a room full of boys and girls you don't know. Not one of your friends is there. Now, imagine that two of the kids walk up to you. They smile and say, "Hi! Would you like to play with us?" You say yes, and soon the room is full of kids that you DO know. If you want to make friends, be friendly to others. Say hi and invite them to play with you. Soon you will have some really good friends.

1. Who are your best friends?
2. What do you like best about your friends?
3. How can a person make a new friend?

> *Dear God,*
> *Thank you for friends. Help me to be friendly to others. Amen.*

Don't Trick People
PROVERBS 26:18-19

A person might be caught lying to his neighbor. And he might say, "I was just fooling." But if he does this, he is like a madman throwing around firebrands, arrows, and death!

PROVERBS 26:18-19

Do you enjoy telling jokes and riddles? It's fun to make people laugh. But sometimes people play tricks on others. They want to laugh AT someone. They want to make someone look silly or feel bad. The Bible says that tricking others is wrong. If you trick people, soon no one will trust you. They will not want to be your friends. Don't play tricks on others just so you can laugh at them. Have fun that doesn't make anyone feel bad.

1. What tricks do kids play on others in your school or neighborhood?
2. When was the last time somebody tricked you? How did it feel?
3. What should a kid do when he or she wants to play a trick on somebody?

Dear God,
You never play tricks on me. So please help me to make jokes that EVERYBODY can laugh at. Amen.

A Verse about Bragging
PROVERBS 27:2

Don't praise yourself. Let others do it.

PROVERBS 27:2

Do you know anyone who likes to brag? Kids who brag tell themselves and everyone else how good they are. Kids who brag think of themselves before others. They always want to be first in line. That's selfish. Kids like that are no fun to be around. Instead of bragging and telling people how good you are, God says to let others praise you. Don't praise yourself. Be humble and let others see your good actions. That's a whole lot better than bragging.

1. What is something nice someone has said about you?
2. How do your friends feel when you praise them?
3. What brother, sister, or friend would you like to praise right now?

Dear God,
Please help me to be humble like Jesus. Show me how to praise others and not myself. Amen.

No More Angry Words
PROVERBS 29:11

A person who can't control his anger is foolish. A person who controls his anger is wise.

PROVERBS 29:11

Let's say you get mad at a friend. Let's say you call that friend a name. Later you forget what happened. But your friend does NOT forget. Later you decide you like your friend after all. But by then it's too late. Your angry words have already hurt your friend's feelings. Once you let an angry word out of your mouth, you can never, ever get it back! That's why God says it is wise to hold your tongue.

1. How do you act when you feel very angry?
2. What are some ways to tell someone you're angry without yelling or calling names?
3. What are some ways you can use words to make people feel good?

Dear God,
    Help me to use my tongue today in ways that please you. Amen.

Be Generous
ISAIAH 32:8

**Good men will be kind to others. They will
be blessed of God for all they do.**

ISAIAH 32:8

You can make something special happen. It can happen when you share your toys. It can happen when you give money to the church. It can even happen when you give a gift. God notices when you share. He sees you being kind and generous with your stuff—your games, your toys, your clothes, your money. God is generous, too. If you give to others, God will be glad. And he will make sure you always have enough.

1. When have you been generous with something that belonged to you?
2. Who has been generous to you?
3. How can you be generous at home?

Dear God,
*   You give me so much. Thank you! Help me*
to share my stuff with others. Amen.

When Hezekiah heard this, he . . . prayed.

ISAIAH 38:2

You can read more about Hezekiah on page 194 of *The Eager Reader Bible*.

King Hezekiah was one of the best kings in the Bible. He really loved God. How do we know? Hezekiah prayed. He spoke with God about the great things God could do. He told God about things that scared him. He asked God to help him solve his problems. Hezekiah knew he needed God, so he prayed. And God helped him a lot. Everybody needs God. Whenever you get scared or want to celebrate or need some help, talk to God.

1. What do you think is neat about Hezekiah's prayer?
2. What sorts of things can people pray about?
3. What do you want to pray about today?

Dear God,
I'm glad you let us pray and talk to you.
Thank you for listening and helping. Amen.

God's Help and Protection
JEREMIAH 7:4-10

You think that because the Temple is here, you will never suffer? Don't fool yourselves!

JEREMIAH 7:8

Some grown-ups have good-luck charms hanging from their car mirror. Some kids wear good-luck charms on a bracelet or necklace. Some people do other things to bring good luck. None of that stuff works. God can take care of us and guide us all the time, everywhere. Who's stronger—a toy rabbit's foot or God? Who's bigger a set of dice on a key chain or God? Don't depend on good-luck charms. Trust in God to help and protect you. He can do it.

1. What good-luck charms have you seen?
2. Why do people think good-luck charms bring them good luck?
3. What would you think if someone started praying to a good-luck charm?

Dear God,
   Because I have you, I don't need good-luck charms. Thank you for helping me every day. I trust in you. Amen.

Stick Up for Others
JEREMIAH 26

Ahikam, the son of Shaphan, stood with Jeremiah. He was the royal secretary. He made sure the court did not turn him over to the mob to kill him.

JEREMIAH 26:24

One day Jeremiah brought some bad news: God was going to destroy the Temple. The people did not like Jeremiah's message. So the city officials got together and talked about killing him! Just then, a man named Ahikam spoke up. "Leave Jeremiah alone!" he said. This was not easy for Ahikam to do. The city officials could have killed him, too. But Jeremiah was in danger, so Ahikam stuck up for him. And it worked. The city officials did not hurt Jeremiah! Stick up for others who need some help.

1. What do you think is neat about what Ahikam did for Jeremiah?
2. How was Ahikam a special friend to Jeremiah?
3. Have you ever stood up for a per son in danger?

Dear God,
Thank you for all my friends. Help me protect them when they need me to. Amen.

[God said,] "A person might be walking on the wrong road and find his mistake. And then he goes back to the fork where he made the wrong turn. But these people keep on going along their evil path. They do this even though I warn them."

JEREMIAH 8:5

You can read more about lonely Jeremiah on page 198 of *The Eager Reader Bible*.

The people of God rebelled against the Lord. Jeremiah tried to warn them. "Turn back to God," Jeremiah said. But nobody wanted to listen to Jeremiah or his warnings. The king of Babylon came to fight God's people with his army. He captured them all and made them his slaves. "This is exactly what I told you would happen," Jeremiah said. Now the people of God wished they had taken Jeremiah's advice. Jeremiah's warning was right. A wise person listens to warnings.

1. Why did Jeremiah warn his people?
2. What makes it hard sometimes to listen to warnings?
3. What kind of warnings do you think are most important?

Dear God,
Please help me to listen to warnings.
Amen.

Don't Pout
EZEKIEL 37

[God said,] "I will make my home among
them. Yes, I will be their God. And they
shall be my people."

EZEKIEL 37:27

What do you do when things don't go your way? Some kids pout. Some stomp and yell. Some cry. But others say, "It's OK. God is taking care of me." One time God's people got taken away from their homes to a country called Babylon. They wondered if they would EVER get to go home. That's when God said, "Don't be sad. I am still with you." When things don't go your way, you don't need to pout or cry. God is taking care of you.

1. What makes you feel like pouting? Why?
2. What's the best part of being a child of God? (Hint: Say what YOU like best about it.)
3. How can you cheer up a friend who is sad?

Dear God,
   I don't want to be a pouter. When things don't go my way, help me to think about the great future you have planned for me. Amen.

Then the king promoted Shadrach, Meshach, and Abednego in the province of Babylon.

DANIEL 3:30

You can read more about Shadrach, Meshach, and Abednego on page 206 of *The Eager Reader Bible*.

The three young men with weird names would not bow to the king's big statue. They prayed only to God, not hunks of metal. Only God deserves to be worshiped. That's the rule, and these men kept it. The king got so mad that he screamed and made threats. And into the furnace went the young men. But God kept them safe. The king was so amazed that even he believed in God! So don't forget rule number one: Worship only God.

1. If you had to face a wicked king, what two friends would you want to have along?
2. How does God help kids in trouble?
3. How can you show everybody that God is first in your heart?

Dear God,
*   I always want to worship you and nothing else. Amen.*

Kidding Around
DANIEL 5

**Oh, the joys of those who . . . do not laugh
at the things of God.**

PSALM 1:1

You can read more about the writing on the wall
on page 210 of *The Eager Reader Bible.*

King Belshazzar's party got out of control. He showed off by serving drinks in gold and silver cups that were stolen from God's Temple. Then the king made fun of God. Suddenly the party stopped. A hand had appeared. It wrote a message on the wall. The message said that the king would soon be punished for making fun of God. And the king died that very night. Never make fun of God, not even for play.

1. What are some things you like to do at parties?

2. Why did the king get in so much trouble?

3. What would you have said to Belshazzar if you were at his party?

Dear God,
You are mighty, awesome, great, and King of all. Please remind me never to make fun of you. Amen.

Prayer
DANIEL 6

**Daniel . . . bowed down as usual in his
upstairs bedroom. He opened its windows
toward Jerusalem. He prayed there three
times a day.**

DANIEL 6:10

You can read more about Daniel and the lions on
page 214 of *The Eager Reader Bible.*

One day the king of the country where Daniel lived made a law that said, "You cannot pray to anyone but the king!" Daniel ignored the law. He went to his window, opened the shutters, and prayed to God every day, three times a day. Daniel knew that it was important. Be like Daniel. Pray every day. Don't go to bed before you pray to the Lord.

1. What do you pray about day after day?
2. When's the best time for you to pray so you always remember and don't forget?
3. What kinds of things do you like to pray about?

Dear God,
Thank you that I can pray. Help me to pray every day. Amen.

A Verse about Blame
Hosea 4:4

"Don't point your finger at someone else!
Don't try to pass the blame to him!"

HOSEA 4:4

Hosea had a hard job to do. God's people were doing bad things. But that's not all. They were blaming it all on others! Hosea told them to stop. Taking the blame IS hard. But saying that someone else really did it doesn't help anything. It is easy to blame your little brother or sister for what you do wrong. But God knows who REALLY is to blame. Be a big kid. Admit it when you do something wrong. Don't blame others.

1. Why do kids sometimes say "It wasn't my fault!" when it really was?
2. What would you do if your mom or dad asked, "Who started it?"
3. What happens to a friendship when blame gets passed around?

Dear God,
    I feel bad when I do something wrong. I'm sorry for when I try to blame other kids. Please help me to be honest and good. Amen.

Confession
JONAH 1—4

God saw that they had put a stop to their evil ways. So he decided not to destroy them.

JONAH 3:10

You can read more about Jonah and the big fish on page 190 of *The Eager Reader Bible.*

W atch out!" Jonah warned. "God will punish you for your sins." The people in the city of Nineveh were sad when they heard Jonah's message. They cried out to God, "Please forgive us!" They stopped doing bad things. God gladly forgave them and did not punish them. God forgives us whenever we say, "I'm sorry, God." God can forgive ANYBODY.

1. Why did God forgive the people of Nineveh?
2. How do you feel when someone says, "I'm sorry"?
3. What's the best way to tell God you're sorry for doing something bad?

Dear God,
I am sorry for my sins. Please forgive me.
Thank you for making it OK. Amen.

Blurting Things Out
LUKE 1:1-25

[Zechariah] said to the angel, "But this is impossible! I'm an old man now. And my wife is also well along in years."

LUKE 1:18

You can read more about Zechariah and the angel on page 230 of *The Eager Reader Bible.*

One day an angel came to Zechariah. He said that Zechariah's wife would soon have a baby. "No way!" Zechariah blurted out. "That can't be!" "I stand in the presence of God," the angel said. He told Zechariah that he would not be able to speak for a while. And Zechariah was not able to speak until the baby was born. It is easy to say the first thing that comes into your head. But it's better to think first.

1. Why did Zechariah get in trouble for what he said?
2. What should Zechariah have done instead of blurting out the first thing he thought?
3. When do you think it's a good idea to think before you speak?

Dear God,
    Sometimes I blurt things out before I should. Please help me to think before I speak. Amen.

The Birth of Jesus
LUKE 1:18—2:23

The Savior has been born tonight in Bethlehem! Yes, this is the Messiah, the Lord!

LUKE 2:11

You can read more about Jesus' birth on page 234 of *The Eager Reader Bible*.

Jesus' parents were not famous people. Jesus wasn't born in a fancy hospital. Why did angels announce his birth? Why did shepherds and the wise men travel a long way to visit a poor little baby? Jesus was no ordinary baby. He was the Son of God. He came into the world to save us from our sins. Jesus came for you, too. If you ask him to be YOUR Savior and Lord, he will!

1. What did the shepherds and the wise men think of Jesus?
2. Why did Jesus have to be born?
3. What do you like best about Jesus?

Dear God,
Thank you for sending your Son, Jesus, to save me from my sins. Amen.

Honoring Jesus
MATTHEW 2:1-12

They went to the house where the baby and Mary, his mother, were. The wise men threw themselves down before him, worshiping. Then they opened the gifts they had brought.

MATTHEW 2:11

You can read more about the wise men's special visit on page 238 of *The Eager Reader Bible.*

When Jesus was a very little boy, wise men came to visit him. The three men came from far, far away. They had followed a star to find Jesus. They carried special presents to share with Jesus. When the three wise men finally found Jesus, they bowed down and worshiped him. They gave Jesus their most precious gifts of gold and spices. They gave Jesus the most valuable things they had. They knew that Jesus deserved it. He deserves our very best.

1. What nice things do you have?
2. Why did the wise men give such valuable gifts to young Jesus?
3. How does God feel when we give or share our special things?

Dear God,
    Thank you for coming to save us. Please help me to give you my very best. Amen.

Go to Church
LUKE 2:41-52

Let us not neglect our church meetings, as some people do. Encourage and warn each other. Do this especially now that his day of coming is near.

HEBREWS 10:25

You can read more about the boy Jesus on page 242 of *The Eager Reader Bible.*

Have you ever been lost? When Jesus was a boy, he and his parents often went to the Temple. They went there to worship God. One day Jesus' parents left the Temple to go home. They thought that Jesus was with their relatives. But he was not. Soon they found him. He was in the Temple talking to the teachers about God. Jesus loved being in God's place of worship. Going to church is one way to be just like Jesus.

1. What is your favorite part of going to church?
2. Who do you like to see at church?
3. Was there ever a time when your mom or dad came to look for you because you were lost?

Dear God,
*   Thank you for my church. Thank you for the people there who love me. Amen.*

Obeying Parents
LUKE 2:41—52

[Jesus] went back to Nazareth with them and obeyed them.

LUKE 2:51

Jesus had to grow up just like every other boy and girl. His mom and dad had rules, too, just like every other mom and dad. Joseph and Mary were in charge at their house. Jesus really wanted to obey his parents. That's why he always followed their rules. Whatever they said, he did. That made them glad. Your parents will be glad when you obey them, too.

1. What do you like and dislike about having your mom or dad in charge?
2. When is it hardest to obey your parents?
3. What can a kid do when he doen't like the rules at home?

Dear God,
Help me to be like Jesus today. Help me to obey my parents. Amen.

[John said], "Prove by the way you live that you really have repented."

LUKE 3:8

You can read more about John the Baptist on page 246 of *The Eager Reader Bible.*

John the Baptist was like an announcer at a ball game. His job was to tell everyone about the coming Savior, Jesus. "Get ready," he told them. "Jesus is coming! Get ready, everybody!" "How can we?" everybody asked. "If you have some extra stuff, share it with others," John said. "Stop calling names. Be kind instead of mean. Be honest and don't steal." Everybody heard. And some of them listened. The ones who really wanted to meet Jesus did what John said. Do you want to meet Jesus someday? Then get ready now!

1. What did John want everybody to do?
2. Who's the most famous person you've ever met?
3. What good deeds have you learned to do because of Jesus?

> *Dear God,*
> *Help me to get ready for Jesus like John told us to do. I want to be ready when Jesus comes back. Amen.*

Read the Bible
MATTHEW 4:1-11

I have thought much about your words. I have stored them in my heart. That way they will hold me back from sin.

PSALM 119:11

You can read more about Jesus being tempted on page 250 of *The Eager Reader Bible.*

Jesus went into a lonely desert to pray. The devil tried his best to make Jesus sin. He tempted Jesus three times. But each time Jesus said no. How did Jesus keep from getting tricked? He knew the Bible. He did not have to wonder, *Should I do what the devil says?* Jesus knew what the Bible said to do. Read the Bible a lot. It will keep you from doing wrong.

1. What are some of your favorite parts of the Bible?
2. When was a time the Bible helped you know what to do?
3. How did knowing the Bible help Jesus?

Dear God,
Thank you for the Bible. Please help me to remember it like Jesus did. Amen.

Getting Help
JOHN 2:1-12

The wine supply ran out during the feast. And Jesus' mother came to him with the problem.

JOHN 2:3

You can read more about Jesus at the wedding party on page 258 of *The Eager Reader Bible*.

Jesus and his mother, Mary, were at a large wedding. It was a wonderful celebration. Lots of people were laughing and having fun. Then the wine ran out. OH, NO! Mary knew just who to ask for help. Mary went to Jesus and told him about the problem. She told the servants to do whatever Jesus said. Jesus told the servants to fill six large jars with water. Then Jesus turned the water into wine. Everyone was glad that Mary had asked Jesus for help.

1. What is the best party you've ever been to? Why?
2. What was Mary not afraid to do?
3. What is something you want to ask Jesus for help with?

> *Dear Jesus,*
>   *Thank you for being able to help me with your great power. Please teach me never to be afraid to ask you for help. Amen.*

Take Care of Your Church
JOHN 2:12-25

[Jesus said,] "Don't turn my Father's house into a market!"

JOHN 2:16

One day Jesus went to the Temple. He wanted to worship God. But instead of finding a quiet place to pray, Jesus found a whole bunch of people selling things. They were not there to worship God. They were there to make money! Jesus made them stop. Today, we go to church instead of the Temple. God really cares about your church. He wants it to be used for worship, not silly or selfish things.

1. Why did Jesus make a whip and turn over the tables of the mer chants?

2. What do you like best about your church?
3. How does your church help you worship God?

Dear God,
   Thank you for my church. Please help me to take good care of it. Amen.

A Verse about Name-calling
MATTHEW 7:1

[Jesus said,] "Don't judge others. Then you won't be judged."

MATTHEW 7:1

Has anyone ever called you dumb or stupid? Lots of people say it. Or maybe they use a name they made up to make you feel bad. Jesus hates that kind of talk. "Don't judge others," he says. "Then they won't judge you." If you call somebody a name, watch out. Maybe they will call you names, too. And then you'll be really mad. So don't call people names no matter how much you want to. Let God do the judging.

1. What's the worst name anyone has ever called you?
2. What would most kids say about Jesus' command?
3. What's wrong with calling a person a name?

Dear Lord,
   It's easy to call people names. Please forgive me and help me not to do that. Amen.

Tell Your Friends
LUKE 5:1-11

Jesus said to them, "Don't be afraid! From now on you'll be fishing for the souls of men!"

LUKE 5:10

You can read more about Jesus and Peter and the fish on page 266 of *The Eager Reader Bible.*

Peter and John enjoyed fishing a lot. But all night they had been skunked. No fish. Then Jesus gave them simple instructions. "Go out deeper, and throw your nets!" And the nets filled up with fish. That was how Jesus showed Peter and John a new kind of fishing: "catching people" for the kingdom of God. That's the plan. Someone tells you about Jesus. Then you tell someone else about Jesus. Then they tell another person. Pretty soon all folks everywhere will have heard about Jesus!

1. Have you ever gone fishing?
2. Which of your friends know Jesus? Who doesn't?
3. Why do your friends need to know about Jesus?

Dear God,
I have some friends who haven't heard about Jesus. Please help me tell them so they'll know you like I do! Amen.

Don't Talk Badly about Others
MARK 2:13-17

Jesus [said,] "Sick people need the doctor, not healthy ones! I haven't come to tell good people to repent. I have come to save the bad ones."

MARK 2:17

You can read more about Jesus and his special friends on page 254 of *The Eager Reader Bible*.

Jesus chose 12 men to be his special followers. Some people were surprised by his choices. "I can't believe it!" they said. "Doesn't Jesus know he is picking sinners?" The truth is that all of us are sinners. We all need the special friendship of Jesus. Don't talk badly about others. The ones who sin the most are the ones who need Jesus the most. Don't bad-mouth bad kids. They need Jesus. Pray for them!

1. What kind of followers did people expect Jesus to pick?
2. What do you think Jesus thought about when he met someone?
3. Do you know someone who needs the special friendship of Jesus?

> *Dear God,*
> *I'm glad that Jesus came to save us. Please help me to pray for the kids who really need him. Amen.*

When Good Happens to Others
JOHN 5:1-15

When others are happy, be happy with them. If they are sad, share their sadness.

ROMANS 12:15

You can read more about Jesus healing the man who could not walk on page 270 of *The Eager Reader Bible*.

Jesus made something wonderful happen. He saw a man sitting by a pool. The man could not walk. Jesus told him to stand up. Right then the man got up and walked about. He was all better! He was very happy. But some folks were not happy. They didn't like Jesus so they gave the man a hard time. Be glad when good things happen to others. Then they will be glad when good things happen to you!

1. When has something good happened to your friends?
2. How can you show someone you are happy for them?
3. Who would you tell first if something wonderful happened to you?

Dear God,
    Sometimes you do really neat things for people. Please help me to be happy for them, even if I'm wishing it happened to me, too.
Amen.

When Someone Is Sad
LUKE 7:11-17

When the Lord saw her, he felt very sorry for her. "Don't cry!" he said.

LUKE 7:13

You can read more about Jesus and the sad woman on page 274 of *The Eager Reader Bible.*

Jesus was a very busy man. He was always moving on to new places and meeting new people. But Jesus always took time to be kind. He took time to help people who were sad. Once he met a woman whose only son had died. Jesus spoke kindly to her and helped her. "Don't cry," he said. (And then he made her son alive again!) Sometimes your friends will be sad. Don't laugh at them. Be kind and see if you can help.

1. Who has helped you when you were sad? How?
2. Pretend that Jesus goes to your school. How would he act if someone started crying?
3. How can you help a friend the next time he or she is sad?

> *Dear God,*
>   *Thank you for caring about me. Please help me to be kind to people who are sad. Amen.*

When You Get Scared
MARK 4:35-41

And [Jesus] asked them, "Why were you so afraid? Don't you have confidence in me yet?"

MARK 4:40

You can read more about Jesus and the disciples in the thunderstorm on page 278 of *The Eager Reader Bible*.

*K*aboom! *Crash! Whoosh!* The violent storm rocked the disciples' little boat. They were really scared. They thought they were going to die. They were so afraid that they forgot to pray. "Wake up, Jesus!" they cried. Jesus was asleep in the boat. Jesus woke up and told the sea to be calm. "Why were you afraid?" Jesus asked. "You can always pray to God when you're afraid."

1. What do you do when you hear thunder and lightning?
2. Why wasn't Jesus afraid of the storm?
3. What can you always do when you're scared?

Dear Jesus,

Please protect me from all my fears. Thank you for always listening to my prayers when I'm scared. Amen.

The Power of Jesus
LUKE 8:26-39

Everyone begged Jesus to go away and leave them alone. For a deep wave of fear had swept over them. So Jesus went back to the boat and left.

LUKE 8:37

You can read more about Jesus helping the wild man on page 282 of *The Eager Reader Bible*.

One day Jesus met a wild man. The man had demons inside him. Jesus made all the demons go away. It was a great miracle. The wild man became a calm, loving man. The man's neighbors did not understand. They were afraid of the power that Jesus had. So they did a very silly thing. They asked Jesus to go away! Don't be afraid of Jesus. He is your friend, and he wants to help.

1. What's your favorite part of the story about Jesus and the wild man?
2. How does it make you feel to know that Jesus is more powerful than any other person or thing in the whole universe?

3. Why do you think some people are afraid of Jesus?

Dear God,
    Thank you that Jesus will never leave me. I want him to stay with me and change me more and more. Amen.

Jesus took the loaves. . . . And the bread was passed out to the people. After that he did the same with the fish. And everyone ate until full!

JOHN 6:11

You can read more about Jesus providing food for thousands of people on page 286 of *The Eager Reader Bible.*

Early in the day, the young boy packed his lunch: two fish, five little hunks of bread, no peanut butter. Just enough for one boy (as long as other kids didn't swipe any). But before he could eat any of it, Jesus asked for it. So the boy gave his lunch away. How could that little lunch feed so many? Well, Jesus made sure that it did. Jesus used the boy's lunch to feed a large, hungry crowd. He always makes things stretch for kids who share.

1. What's your favorite kind of sandwich? cookie? vegetable?
2. How can you share food with kids who don't have enough?
3. Why is sharing food a good way of helping kids know more about Jesus?

Dear God,
Help me share with people who are hungry.
Amen.

Praying Alone
MATTHEW 14:22-33

Jesus went up into the hills to pray.

MATTHEW 14:23

You can read more about Jesus praying alone
on page 290 of *The Eager Reader Bible*.

Sometimes Jesus prayed with other people. But one day he decided to pray to God by himself. So he found a quiet spot up on a hill and started to pray. Jesus knew he could talk to God about anything. He could pray ANYWHERE, and God would listen. Before long it was nighttime. Jesus was still praying. It was nearly four o'clock in the morning when Jesus stopped! Jesus enjoyed spending time alone with God. Do you?

1. What sorts of things do you pray about?
2. Where could you find a special
place to be alone with God?
3. When can you pray to God?

Dear God,
    Thank you for listening to all my secret prayers. Amen.

Then Peter came to Jesus. "Sir, how often should I forgive a brother who sins against me?" he asked. "Should I forgive him seven times?" "No!" Jesus replied, "seventy times seven!"

MATTHEW 18:21-22

A servant owed a LOT of money to his master. The servant begged for mercy. And the master said, "OK—you owe me nothing." Then the servant went away and found a person who owed him just a LITTLE bit of money. The servant said, "Pay me right NOW!" The master was angry at the servant. He should have been kind about the little debt. Always forgive others because God has forgiven you.

1. Why did the master forgive the servant?
2. Why didn't the servant forgive the person's little debt?
3. What things have your family or friends forgiven you for?

Dear God,
   Thank you for forgiving my sins. Help me to forgive other people and really mean it. Amen.

Good Neighbors
LUKE 10:25-37

[Jesus] answered, "You must love the Lord your God with all your heart. . . . And you must love your neighbor just as much as you love yourself."

LUKE 10:27

You can read more about he parable of the good neighbor on page 294 of *The Eager Reader Bible.*

Jesus once told a story about a man who was attacked by robbers. The robbers beat him up and left him to die. Two other men came along soon after. But they did not help the hurt man. They just ignored him. A third man came along and said, "Oh! Look what has happened! I must help him." And he did. Does your brother have trouble with math? Is your mom too tired to sweep the floor? Be kind and help any way you can.

1. Why do you think people would not stop to help a hurt person?
2. How can you help others at home? at church? at school?
3. What are some ways your family can help people you don't know?

Dear God,
   Thank you for making me strong and able. Please teach me how to help others whenever I can. Amen.

Listening
LUKE 10:38-42

[Martha's] sister Mary sat on the floor. She listened to Jesus as he talked.

LUKE 10:39

You can read more about Mary and Martha on page 298 of *The Eager Reader Bible.*

Martha was very mad. Jesus and his disciples came over for dinner, and there was lots of work to do. All her sister, Mary, did was sit at Jesus' feet and listen to him speak. Martha had to do all the work by herself. Martha blurted out, "Jesus! Tell Mary to help with all this work. I'm doing it ALL BY MYSELF." But Jesus said that Mary was doing the right thing. Martha learned that listening to Jesus is more important than anything.

1. What is your least favorite chore in the whole world?
2. Why was Martha so upset with Mary?
3. Why did Jesus want Martha to calm down?

Dear God,
*   Please help me to listen closely whenever someone is teaching about God. Amen.*

Thinking of Others
LUKE 14:7-14

[Jesus said,] "Everyone who tries to honor himself will be humbled. And he who humbles himself will be honored."

LUKE 14:11

You can read more about bragging and boasting on page 306 of *The Eager Reader Bible.*

Jesus often told people to behave just the opposite of the way we normally would. At a football game, don't push and shove for the best seat. Take the end zone. At a party, don't gobble all the treats. Let others have some. At school, don't hang around cool kids all day. Make friends with some nerdy ones. When you win a prize, don't brag about yourself. Be humble and talk about the trophies your friends have won.

1. Why is it hard not to brag if you've done something special?
2. Why does Jesus want us to give the spotlight to others?
3. What's the best thing to do when you get tired of hearing someone brag?

Dear God,
    Please help me brag about others and not myself. Amen.

Lost Sheep
LUKE 15:1-7

[Jesus said,] "There is great joy in Heaven over one lost sinner who comes back to God."

LUKE 15:7

You can read more about the lost sheep on page 310 of *The Eager Reader Bible*

Imagine that you are a shepherd. One day one of your sheep gets lost. You look and look for it. And when you find it, you are VERY glad! God cares for every person the way a shepherd cares for every sheep. When a kid acts bad and starts trouble, he's like a lost sheep. God is sad and wants him to come back. And when the kid starts to obey God, he's like a sheep coming home. God is very happy indeed!

1. When was a time you got lost, and who found you?
2. Who would look for you if you ever got lost?

3. How does it feel to know that God cares so much for you?

Dear God,
    Thank you for caring so much for every single kid. Please keep looking for the ones who are like lost sheep. Amen.

Think of Others
Luke 15:11-32

[Love] is never . . . selfish or rude. Love does not demand its own way.

1 CORINTHIANS 13:5

You can read more about the lost son and his brother on page 314 of *The Eager Reader Bible*.

Have you ever heard the story of the Prodigal Son? A young man left home, never to return. But he soon spent all his money. So he changed his mind and went back home. His father gave him a huge welcome-home party. The older brother got very mad. "Why don't you give ME a party?" he demanded. Sometimes other people get what you always wanted. Don't be jealous. Be glad for the other person.

1. Why did the father give a party for the younger brother?
2. When do you get jealous of some one else?
3. What kind of party can you put on for your brother or sister?

Dear God,
    Sometimes I think only of myself. Please help me to think of others, too. Amen.

Feeling Superior
LUKE 16:19-31

Don't be selfish. Don't live to impress others. Be humble. Think of others as better than yourself.

PHILIPPIANS 2:3

Jesus told a story about a rich man. The rich man thought his big house and nice clothes made him great. He thought he was way more important than his poor neighbor Lazarus. In fact, he would not go anywhere near Lazarus. He locked the gate so Lazarus could not get in. But Jesus said that was a big mistake. Every person is important, even people who are poor or sick. Don't feel superior. Lend a hand.

1. Why did the rich man think he was better than Lazarus?
2. Why do some people brag about their things?
3. What's one way kids can include all kinds of other kids in their games and activities?

Dear God,
    Thank you for your many blessings. Please help me to be glad for them and to share them, not to brag about them. Amen.

Comfort
JOHN 11:1-44

Comfort those who are afraid.

1 THESSALONIANS 5:14

You can read more about Jesus comforting Mary and Martha on page 302 of *The Eager Reader Bible.*

Whenever you feel sad, remember three things from the story of Jesus and Lazarus. First, sadness is a part of life. Until we get to heaven, sad things will keep happening because of sin. Second, Jesus knows how you feel. When his friend Lazarus died, Jesus was so upset that he cried. Third, Jesus can change your sadness into happiness. Jesus wants to comfort you when you're sad. He wants you to remember that he loves you. He is always with you—no matter what happens.

1. Why do people get sad at funerals?
2. What makes you sad? What makes you happy?
3. How can you comfort a friend when he or she is sad?

Dear God,
   Thank you for comforting me when I am sad. Help me to comfort others too. Amen.

Saying Thank You
LUKE 17:11-19

[The healed man] fell flat on the ground in front of Jesus. His face was down in the dust. He thanked Jesus for what he had done.

LUKE 17:16

Ten sick men came to Jesus. Jesus healed them all. But only one sick man said thank you to Jesus. The other nine thought only about being healed. They did not go back to tell Jesus thanks. That made Jesus sad. We are like the 10 sick men. We receive lots of good things from God. Then we get excited about those things. Sometimes we forget to say thank you to God. Let's be sure to thank God for all the blessings he gives us, because he has been very kind!

1. What gift or present have you gotten excited about?
2. How do you feel when someone says thank you?

3. What are you thankful for right now?

Dear God,
I want to thank you for _____,
_____, and _____. You are generous
and good! Amen.

Showing Off
LUKE 18:9-14

[Jesus said,] "The corrupt tax collector stood at a distance. He did not even dare to lift his eyes to Heaven as he prayed. . . . He said, 'God, be merciful to me, a sinner!'"

LUKE 18:13

You can read more about the two men who prayed on page 318 of *The Eager Reader Bible*.

Two men went to the Temple to pray. One was a leader. The other was a tax collector. Everyone hated tax collectors because they cheated people. The leader prayed like this: "O God, I am a good person. I'm not like that bad tax collector over there!" But the tax collector didn't brag about how good he was. He just asked God to forgive him. He was really sorry for his sins. He knew that everybody needs God's help.

1. What did the leader do wrong?
2. What did the tax collector do right?
3. How does God want us to pray?

Dear Lord,
   Thank you for loving me. I'm glad you forgive me. Please help me not to brag about myself when I pray. Amen.

Little Kids
MARK 10:13-16

Jesus saw what was happening. And he was very much upset with his disciples. He said to them, "Let the children come to me. For the Kingdom of God belongs to such as they. Don't send them away!"

MARK 10:14

You can read more about Jesus and the children on page 322 of *The Eager Reader Bible*.

264

Babies sure get a lot of attention. They fuss and cry. They have to be watched all the time. You may think, *Why make such a big fuss over such a little person?* It's because God cares a lot about little ones. A song you may know says, "Jesus loves the little children, ALL the children of the world." That song tells the truth. We should look out for little babies and little kids, too, because God thinks they're super important.

1. What are some silly things babies and small children do?
2. How does it make you feel to know that Jesus especially loves children?
3. What would you tell Jesus if you could sit on his lap right now?

Dear God,
I am glad you love little children. Please help me to look out for the little kids around my neighborhood. Amen.

Being Bossy
MARK 10:46-52

"Shut up!" some of the people yelled at him.
But he only shouted the louder, again and
again. "O Son of David!" he cried. "Have
mercy on me!"

MARK 10:48

You can read more about the blind man being
healed on page 326 of *The Eager Reader Bible*.

When the blind man yelled to Jesus, people nearby got bossy. "Shut up!" they said. "You're making a lot of noise. Leave Jesus alone." What if the blind man had listened? Jesus might never have noticed him! Don't be bossy. Telling someone to shut up is like saying, "I don't care about you at all. You don't count for anything." But Jesus wants us to respect people. That's what HE does.

1. Do you know someone who makes too much noise?
2. What is a nice way you could ask someone to be quiet?
3. If someone tells you to shut up, what should you say back?

Dear God,
    Help me not to be bossy. I know I shouldn't say "Shut up" to people. I'll try harder to respect them. Amen.

Cheating
LUKE 19:1-10

Zacchaeus stood before the Lord. He said, "Sir, . . . I might find I have charged someone too much for his taxes. If so, I will give him back four times as much as I took!"

LUKE 19:8

You can read more about Zacchaeus on page 330 of *The Eager Reader Bible*.

Zacchaeus got rich by cheating. His job was to collect tax money from people. But he always took more money than he was supposed to. He kept the extra money for himself. Then one day he met Jesus. Jesus told him that cheating was wrong. Zacchaeus was sorry that he had cheated people. So he promised to pay back all he stole, plus more. Jesus was very glad. And Zacchaeus felt filled with joy. It is better to be honest than to be a cheater.

1. Why do you think Zacchaeus paid back more money than he stole?
2. How would you give back the stolen money if you were Zacchaeus?

3. What does it mean to be fair (and not cheat) in some of your favorite games?

Dear God,
*   I don't want to be a cheater. Please make me a fair and honest person through and through, just like you did for Zacchaeus.*
Amen.

Give to God
JOHN 12:1-11

Honor the Lord by giving him the first part of all your income. Then he will fill your barns with wheat and barley. Your wine vats will overflow with the finest wines.

PROVERBS 3:9-10

You can read more about Mary's present on page 334 of *The Eager Reader Bible.*

Give to God," says the Bible. "Give him the best part of what you have. Don't keep it all to yourself." Helping other people or serving at church are ways to give to God. You can also put some of your allowance in the offering plate. Mary gave to God when she poured perfume on Jesus' feet. And God was pleased. Give some of what you have. Give and you will be blessed.

1. How has God given to you?
2. Who is the most giving person you know?
3. What do you have to give? (Hint: Think of money, toys, and jobs you can do.)

Dear God,
   Thank you for all you have given to me. Show me how I can give to you. Amen.

Don't Be Greedy (Like Judas)
JOHN 12:1-11

The lazy person wishes for many things. But his hands refuse to work. He is greedy to get. But the godly love to give!

PROVERBS 21:25-26

You can read more about Mary's present on page 334 of *The Eager Reader Bible.*

Jesus was alone with his best friends. He knew that he was going to die soon. Mary wanted to show him how much she loved him. What could she do? She poured beautiful perfume on his feet! Jesus was thankful. Judas got very upset. He said they could have sold the perfume. Then they could have given the money to poor people. But Judas REALLY wanted the money for himself. He was very greedy. Mary had the right idea. Give and don't be greedy.

1. What was Judas so upset about?
2. Why did Jesus like what Mary did?
3. What is it easy for you to feel greedy about?

Dear God,
Please help me not to be greedy. Help me to be like Mary, not like Judas. Amen.

The crowds pushed on ahead and pressed along behind. They shouted, "God bless King David's Son! God's Man is here! Bless him, Lord! Praise God in highest Heaven!"

MATTHEW 21:9

You can read more about the first Palm Sunday on page 338 of *The Eager Reader Bible.*

Jesus came riding into town on a donkey. Huge crowds of excited people gathered all around Jesus. The people cheered and shouted for Jesus. The people surrounded him just like a hero. All these people wanted a hero. A very special hero like Jesus. Jesus was their hero. The people knew that Jesus came from God. Jesus came to teach the people about God's love. That's why Jesus was their hero. He can be your hero, too!

1. Who is your favorite hero?
2. What do heroes do that make them so important?
3. What kinds of things did Jesus do to be a hero?

Dear Jesus,
    I want you to be my favorite hero. Please help me always to cheer and clap for you. Amen.

[Jesus] poured water into a basin and began to wash the disciples' feet. He wiped them with the towel he had around him.

JOHN 13:5

You can read more about Jesus washing the disciples' feet on page 342 of *The Eager Reader Bible.*

There were no tennis shoes in Bible days—only sandals. There were no sidewalks either—only dusty roads. If you think that there were lots of dirty feet walking around, you are right! Everybody had to wash their feet as soon as they got home. One day Jesus washed the dirty feet of his disciples. He wanted to show them how important it is to help others. Jesus said, "I want you to serve and help each other. If you do, God will bless you."

1. Why would it be yucky to wash someone's dirty feet?

2. How do you think the disciples felt when Jesus started washing their feet?

3. What are some ways you can serve and help someone today?

Dear God,
*   You did some yucky jobs for people. Help me to do yucky jobs for others, too. Amen.*

Become Jesus' Friend
JOHN 15:15

[Jesus said,] "I no longer call you slaves. For a master doesn't confide in his slaves. Now you are my friends. This is proved by the fact that I have told you all that the Father told me."

JOHN 15:15

Did you know that Jesus is looking for friends? Jesus wants to be everyone's friend, but some people don't want to be his friend. Everybody needs a friend like Jesus. He is the best friend you could ever have. Jesus is a very special friend. He loves you more than anyone else. He always keeps secrets. He always keeps his promises, too. Jesus will never hurt your feelings. He is always kind and gentle. Will you be Jesus' friend?

1. What do you like best about your friends?
2. What do you and your friends laugh about?
3. How can you be a good friend to Jesus?

> *Dear Jesus,*
> *You are the best friend I could ever have.*
> *Please help me always to be a good friend to*
> *you. Amen.*

Doing the Right Thing
LUKE 22:39-46

[Jesus] told them, "Pray to God that you will not give in to temptation."

LUKE 22:40

You can read more about Jesus and the disciples praying in the garden on page 350 of *The Eager Reader Bible*.

Jesus' disciples sat down in the garden. They were very tired. Jesus told them to stay awake and to pray for him. But the disciples went to sleep instead. The disciples wanted to do what was right. But they needed God's help to do it. Ask God for help when you have a hard time doing the right thing. He understands and will always help you.

1. What would you have done if you were one of the sleepy disciples?
2. When do you think it is really hard to do the right thing?
3. How should a kid pray when he or she feels tempted?

Dear God,
   I want to do what is right. But sometimes it's hard. Please help me be strong to do the right thing. Amen.

Friendship
Matthew 26:1—27:10

[Jesus] told them, "My soul is crushed with sadness. I am at the point of death. Please stay here. Stay awake with me."

Matthew 26:38

You can read more about Jesus and his friends in the garden on page 354 of *The Eager Reader Bible*.

Jesus was about to die. He knew that Judas had betrayed him. He knew that he would be arrested and killed for crimes he did not commit. He wanted his friends to stay with him. Soon the guards did come. They arrested Jesus and took him away. But Jesus' friends ran away. Do you want to be a good friend? Be ready for some hard times. Stick by your friends when they really need you.

1. Who are your really good friends?
2. Have you and your friends gone through any hard times together?
3. What do friends like most about you?

Dear God,
   Help me to be a good friend to you and to others. Amen.

Don't Fight People
LUKE 22:47-53

Don't stand against violence! If you are slapped on one cheek, turn the other one, too. . . . There is a saying, "Love your friends and hate your enemies." But I say love your enemies, too! Pray for those who treat you badly!

MATTHEW 5:39, 43-44

You can read more about Jesus' arrest on page 354 of *The Eager Reader Bible*.

Jesus and his friends were in a garden. Suddenly soldiers came to arrest him! Some of Jesus' friends got ready to fight. One of them drew his sword and attacked. "Stop!" said Jesus. "Stop fighting!" Jesus let himself get arrested. He knew it was OK. That was what God wanted. That was God's will for him. Jesus didn't want his friends to fight when he got arrested. He doesn't want us to fight with people, either.

1. Why did Jesus' friends want to fight?
2. How can kids solve problems without fighting?
3. What can you do the next time someone starts a fight with you?

Dear God,
   Sometimes people make me mad, and I want to fight back. I'm sorry. Please help me to work it out instead. Amen.

Say You Know Jesus
LUKE 22:54-65

Jesus turned and looked at Peter. Then Peter remembered what he had said: "Before the rooster crows tomorrow morning, you will deny me three times." And Peter walked out of the courtyard, crying bitterly.

LUKE 22:61-62

You can read more about Peter turning his back on Jesus on page 358 of *The Eager Reader Bible*.

Peter said that he would always be Jesus' friend. Peter said he would NEVER turn his back on Jesus. But one night, some folks asked Peter if he was Jesus' friend. Three times Peter said, "I don't know Jesus. I am not his friend." Peter was too scared to admit the truth. Peter became very sad when he thought about what he had done. He cried and cried. He decided never again to hide the fact that he followed Jesus. It's OK to let people know you are a Christian.

1. Who are your favorite friends?
2. How do you think Jesus felt when Peter turned his back on him?
3. What would you say if a kid looked at you and said, "Hey, do YOU know Jesus?"

Dear Jesus,
   Thank you for being my friend. Please help me never to turn my back on you. Amen.

Don't Go Along with Wrong
LUKE 23:13-25

Pilate . . . wanted to set Jesus free. But they shouted louder and louder for Jesus' death. . . . So Pilate sentenced Jesus to die as they demanded.

LUKE 23:20, 23-24

You can read more about Jesus' trial on page 362 of *The Eager Reader Bible*.

Governor Pilate knew that Jesus was a good man. But the angry crowd kept yelling, "No! Don't let him go! Kill him!" The longer Pilate listened, the more scared he got. Finally he did what the people wanted. He ordered the soldiers to kill Jesus, even though he knew it was wrong. Don't be like Governor Pilate. Be brave and stand up for what is right.

1. Why did Governor Pilate go along with the crowd?
2. How can we tell if something is right or wrong?
3. What kind of wrong things do kids pressure other kids to do?

Dear God,
    I don't want to be like Pilate. Help me to do what is right no matter what others tell me. Amen.

Showing Off
LUKE 23:1-49

**One of the criminals hanging beside [Jesus]
. . . said, "So you're the Messiah, are you?
Prove it by saving yourself! And save us,
too, while you're at it!"**

LUKE 23:39

You can read more about the thieves on the cross
on page 366 of *The Eager Reader Bible*.

Two thieves hung on crosses, with Jesus between them. One thief admitted his wrong and asked Jesus to forgive him. But the other admitted nothing. He only wanted Jesus to do a miracle that would get him out of trouble. He dared Jesus to act like God. But Jesus knew why he was on the cross. He knew he had to die so that you and everyone else who believes in him could have eternal life. So Jesus ignored the dare and did what was right. He knew it's never smart to show off.

1. What do kids dare each other to do?
2. When is it right to ignore a dare?
3. What happens when a kid takes a dare to do something bad?

Dear God,
    Sometimes kids dare me to do foolish things. When that happens, please give me the courage to say "Forget it!" Amen.

It's OK to Cry
LUKE 23:1-49

**When the crowd saw that Jesus was dead
they went home very sad.**

LUKE 23:48

You can read more about Jesus' death
on page 366 of *The Eager Reader Bible.*

A crowd of people began to cry when Jesus died. Some remembered his stories. Others thought about how much he loved them. Their memories of Jesus made them very sad. Joseph and Nicodemus buried Jesus later that afternoon. They, too, were sad. They did not want to say good-bye to their dear friend. Jesus' friends and family cried together. Their tears showed how much they loved Jesus. It's OK to cry at times like that.

1. Why was everyone so sad when Jesus died?
2. When was a time you really missed someone who died or went away?

3. When you're crying, what helps you feel better?

Dear God,
It's no fun to cry. But you are with me, and I'm really glad about that. When I cry, please help me to feel better. Amen.

Jesus Is Alive!
MATTHEW 28

The women ran from the tomb. They were afraid, but also filled with joy. They rushed to find the disciples to give them the angel's message.

MATTHEW 28:8

You can read more about Jesus' empty tomb on page 374 of *The Eager Reader Bible.*

Mary and her friends were SO surprised. The giant rock in front of Jesus' tomb had been rolled away. There were angels there. "Jesus is no longer dead," they said. "He is alive!" What awesome news! All that Jesus had said was true. They would see him again; they would have their sins forgiven, and they would get to be in heaven someday. Now they had something to tell and something to celebrate. And so do we!

1. What made Mary and her friends run so fast?
2. What do your friends know about Jesus?
3. What can you tell your friends about Jesus?

Dear God,
 I am so glad that Jesus rose from the dead. Please show my friends that they can know Jesus, too. Amen.

Knowing the Bible
LUKE 24:13-35

Then Jesus said to them, "You are such foolish, foolish people! You find it so hard to believe all that the prophets wrote in the Scriptures!"

LUKE 24:25

You can read more about the two disciples on page 378 of *The Eager Reader Bible*.

Two disciples of Jesus were very sad. They forgot what God promised about Jesus. They thought Jesus was gone forever. The two disciples were in for a big surprise. They were walking along the road. A man met them. He showed them what the Bible said about Jesus. He reminded them that Jesus would become alive again. And then they saw—it was Jesus himself talking to them! The Bible was true! They learned how important it is to believe God's Word.

1. What was God's big surprise for the two disciples?
2. What is your favorite Bible story?
3. What do you learn from Bible stories?

Dear God,
Thank you for all the great promises in the Bible. Please help me to study the Bible so I can remember your promises. Amen.

Jesus Is Alive—Celebrate!
JOHN 20:1-29

[Jesus] said to Thomas, "Put your finger
into my hands. Put your hand into my side.
Don't be faithless any longer. Believe!"

JOHN 20:27

You can read more about Jesus rising from the
dead on page 382 of *The Eager Reader Bible.*

What do you say when something great happens? Do you say "Cool!" or "Awesome!" or "All right!"? Three days after Jesus died, the disciples found out that he had risen from the dead. He appeared to them and talked with them. He told them to tell the whole world about him. He promised to be with them always. No longer were they confused or scared. No longer were they sad and discouraged. Jesus is alive forever! What a reason to celebrate!

1. Why do you think Thomas doubted that Jesus had risen from the dead?
2. How does it make you feel to know that Jesus is alive and with you always?
3. When do we celebrate Jesus becoming alive again? (Hint: It's a holiday at your church.)

> *Dear God,*
> *I praise you for raising Jesus from the dead. I want to celebrate like Jesus' disciples did! Amen.*

[Jesus said,] "I no longer call you slaves. For a master doesn't confide in his slaves. Now you are my friends."

JOHN 15:15

You can read more about Jesus having breakfast with his disciples on page 386 of *The Eager Reader Bible*.

Jesus was saying good-bye to his disciples. He was sad to go. But he wanted to tell them something. He sat down by the lake and had breakfast with them. "I have to go away," he said. "But I will always be your friend. Will you be mine?" They promised they would. And later he sent the Holy Spirit to be with them while he was gone. Jesus wants to be your friend, too.

1. Who are some of your best friends? Why?
2. What do good friends do together?
3. What can you and Jesus do
   together?

> *Dear God,*
> *Thank you for sending Jesus to be my friend. I want to be his friend, too. Amen.*

Your Mission
Acts 1:1-13

[Jesus said,] "Make disciples in all the nations. . . . Teach these new disciples to obey all the commands I have given you. And be sure of this thing! I am with you always, even to the end of the world."

MATTHEW 28:19-20

You can read more about Jesus' last day on earth on page 390 of *The Eager Reader Bible.*

It was the last day Jesus would be on earth. He was going back home to heaven. He took his disciples to a hillside. There he gave them a mission. "Tell other people about me," he said. "Teach them what I taught you." Then he went back to heaven. The disciples worked hard to do what Jesus said. They told many people about Jesus. Some of them wrote down what Jesus had done. That's why YOU know about him. But the job is not finished. More people need to know. Now it is YOUR turn. You have a mission!

1. Who first told you about Jesus? How?
2. What is the first thing you would tell a friend about Jesus?
3. What friends can you talk to about Jesus?

Dear God,
*   Thank you for letting me have a part in your mission. Please help me spread the Good News so my friends will know all about you. Amen.*

Sharing
ACTS 2:42-47

All the believers met together constantly. And they shared everything they had with each other.

ACTS 2:44

You can read more about the first church on page 394 of *The Eager Reader Bible.*

After Jesus rose from the dead, his friends spread the news. More and more people found out that Jesus was the Savior. The new believers met to worship and pray. They shared their food, clothes, and other things, too. They were learning a new way to treat each other. God gives us all that we have. He wants us to share with others. We won't run out just because we give a few things away.

1. Why did the first people who believed in Jesus share so much?
2. When is it hard to share?
3. What kinds of things can you share?

Dear God,
*   You have given me lots of nice things. Help me to share them with others who don't have as much as I do. Amen.*

Helping
Acts 3:1-11

Peter said, "We don't have any money for you! But I'll give you something else! I command you in the name of Jesus Christ of Nazareth, walk!"

ACTS 3:6

You can read more about the healing of the lame man on page 398 of *The Eager Reader Bible*.

One day Peter and John met a poor man who could not walk. The poor man wanted money. Peter and John didn't have any. But Peter did have the power to help in another way. Jesus gave Peter the power to heal people. So Peter healed the poor man and made him able to walk. Maybe you don't have any money. Maybe you can't heal people. But you can always help in some way. Do whatever you can to help people.

1. How did Peter and John help the man?
2. What is one way you like to help others?
3. Who is someone who helps you a lot?
4. What are ways God helps people?
5. How can you be God's super helper today?

Dear God,
  Thank you for the people who help me. Please show me how to help others with the things I can do. Amen.

Making New Friends
ACTS 9:1-19

Ananias went over and found Saul and laid his hands on him. "Brother Saul," he said, "the Lord Jesus spoke to you on the road. And now he has sent me so that you may be filled with the Holy Spirit. I have also come to give you your sight back."

ACTS 9:17

Ananias was scared. God told him to go help Paul (Saul). But Paul HATED Christians! Ananias worried that Paul would hurt him or even kill him. But God said, "Go!" So Ananias obeyed. He found out that God had changed Paul. Ananias and Paul even became friends! Ananias learned that God can change anybody—even the most rotten person in the world. Don't give up on anybody.

1. When was a time you didn't want to do something the Bible tells you to do?
2. Who are some people you know who seem to hate God or Jesus?
3. What person would you like to go see and give special help to?

Dear God,
You are so great that you can change anybody. Some kids don't love Jesus. Please help them to change. Amen.

Open Arms
ACTS 10:9-48

Peter [said,] "I see that the Jews are not the only people God loves!"

ACTS 10:34

You can read more about Cornelius and Peter on page 406 of *The Eager Reader Bible.*

Peter was fussy about the people he picked for his friends. Cornelius had some habits Peter didn't like. Cornelius was from a family that Peter didn't like. Cornelius had a job that Peter didn't like. But Jesus told Peter to make friends with Cornelius because Cornelius was one of God's people—just like Peter. So Peter, who loved Jesus most of all, went to visit Cornelius and be his friend. Try to be friendly to all of God's people. We all have Jesus in common.

1. Are there kids at your school or in your neighborhood who are different from you in some way?
2. Why is it important to make friends with people who are different?
3. Who is someone a little different that you could invite over to play?

> *Dear God,*
> *Please help me to be really friendly, and not just to people like myself. Amen.*

Singing
ACTS 16:16-40

Around midnight, Paul and Silas were praying and singing hymns to the Lord. And all the other prisoners were listening to them.

ACTS 16:25

You can read more about Paul and Silas singing in jail on page 410 of *The Eager Reader Bible*.

Paul and Silas were preachers. They told people about Jesus. But some people didn't like that. So they got Paul and Silas thrown in jail. Paul and Silas didn't want to be in jail. They had done nothing wrong. It was cold and dark in there. But they knew Jesus was with them. And they knew he was in charge. So they sang praise songs to God. People who know Jesus can sing no matter WHAT goes wrong.

1. Why were Paul and Silas singing in jail?
2. What songs do you like to sing about Jesus?
3. What songs can you sing the next time everything goes wacko?

Dear God,
    You make me feel like singing. I praise you for being so good to me. Amen.

What to Do If You Get Cheated
ROMANS 8:28-29

Everything that happens to us is working for our good. We know this is true if we love God and fit into his plans.

ROMANS 8:28

If you listen hard, you will sometimes hear adults say, "Life isn't fair." Some kids feel that way, too. Maybe their mom and dad got divorced. Or their kid sister has cancer. Or they can't wrestle or play ball because they got hurt. Or their parents are so poor they don't get anything for Christmas. Don't worry. God has a big plan that'll turn it all into good. He'll even make your unfair hurts turn out OK.

1. What seems unfair to you?
2. If you could make the world more fair, how would you do it?
3. What's the best kind of prayer for a kid who feels cheated?

Dear God,
I can't make people be fair to me. But I'm glad you're in charge anyway. Please work it out so that the unfair stuff turns out OK. Amen.

Making Peace
ROMANS 12:18

Don't argue with anyone. Be at peace with everyone as much as you can.

ROMANS 12:18

Some kids like to pick fights. They tease you. They try to make you hit them back. They take your stuff and make you come get it. They say things that make you angry. Some kids like to argue. They fight with words, not fists. "Nah, nah!" they like to say. If someone tries to pick a fight with you, you don't have to fight. You can talk to them with peaceful words. Be calm. It may be hard at first, but you can learn.

1. What's the meanest thing anyone has ever done to you?
2. When was the last time you wanted to fight somebody?
3. What can a kid do to help stop a fight?

Dear God,
  You like peace more than fighting. Help me to stay out of fights. Amen.

Obey the People in Charge
ROMANS 13:1-7

Obey the rulers because God is the one who has put them there. There are no rulers anywhere that God has not put in power.

ROMANS 13:1

Do you know what a *ruler* is? Police officers, moms and dads, and teachers are rulers. Kings and prime ministers and presidents are rulers, too. God puts these people in charge. He gives them the right to say "Stop speeding!" or "It's time to clean your room!" or "Have you done your homework?" God wants us to obey our rulers so that everything will go smoothly.

1. Who's in charge at your house?
2. How do kids benefit from adults being in charge?
3. What ruler do you have trouble obeying? Why?

Dear God,
*   Thank you for choosing people to be in charge. Please remind me to obey them. Amen.*

Patience
EPHESIANS 4:2

Be humble and gentle. Be patient with each
other. Allow for each other's faults because
of your love.

EPHESIANS 4:2

Don't you just hate it when you have to wait for people? "Hurry up!" you say. "I've been waiting so long!" You wait and you wait and you wait. They take forever! Sometimes people don't do things as quickly as you want them to. God wants us to be patient with them. He wants us to wait anyway, even though we don't want to. He wants us to wait without saying, "Hurry up!"

1. What sort of waiting bugs you the most?
2. Who is the most patient person you know?
3. What can you do (instead of gripping) when you're waiting?

Dear God,
    Teach me to be patient with friends and family. Help me wait for them even when I don't want to. Amen.

Don't Hold a Grudge
EPHESIANS 4:26

If you are angry, don't sin by staying angry.
Don't let the sun go down with you still
angry. Get over it quickly.

EPHESIANS 4:26

Do you know what a grudge is? A grudge is when you get angry at someone and never stop being angry. You get so angry you want to stay angry. You stay angry for a long time because you are really, really mad. That's a grudge. Do you know what grudges do? They mess up our friendships and make God sad. They also make US feel bad. So God says, "Don't stay angry! Instead, forgive!"

1. When do you get mad for a short time, and when do you get mad for a long time?
2. How do kids show it when they forgive each other?
3. What do you like best about what happens when you stop being angry at a friend?

> *Dear God,*
> *I'm glad you have given me family and friends. Please help me to forgive them when they make me mad and not to stay angry with them. Amen.*

A Verse about Bad Words
EPHESIANS 4:29

Don't use bad language. Say only what is good and helpful to those you are talking to. That will give them a blessing.

EPHESIANS 4:29

Here's a way to be good, as God is: Say good words, not dirty words. Tell good stories, not dirty ones. Saying bad words or saying God's name in a bad way hurts God's feelings. It's not the kind of thing that God would do, so neither should we. Say things that help people. If a friend does something neat, say so! If you learn something neat about God, speak up! That's the kind of talk God likes.

1. What kind of talk does God like?
2. When is it easy to use bad words?
3. Why do you think some people talk dirty?

Dear God,
    Thank you for all your goodness to me and my family. Please help me to use good, encouraging words. Amen.

Don't Tell Dirty Jokes
EPHESIANS 5:4

Dirty stories, foul talk, and coarse jokes are not for you. Instead, remind each other of God's goodness and be thankful.

EPHESIANS 5:4

Some people like to say bad words. They tell dirty jokes and then laugh. But do you know what? When we talk ugly like that, God doesn't laugh. Dirty stories make him sad. He wants us to use our mouths to say good things. You don't have to say bad words to be funny. You can laugh and have fun in lots of other ways. By not talking ugly, you make God happy!

1. Why do you think people say so many bad words?
2. What are some words that are OK to say when you get hurt?
3. Who do you know who tells *good* funny stories?

Dear God,
 Please help me to use my mouth to say good words and not bad ones. I want to please you. Amen.

Hiding Bad Deeds
EPHESIANS 5:11

Take no part in the worthless pleasures of
evil and darkness. Instead, rebuke them and
bring them out into the light.

EPHESIANS 5:11

Have you ever hidden a doll or toy under your bedcovers? In the same way, sometimes people try to "cover up" the bad things they do. They want to be sure no one sees what they do wrong. God says never to cover up the bad things people do. Instead, he wants their covers ripped off. God doesn't want anyone to hide any bad deed. God can see everything. Even hidden things. Don't cover for bad people—take off their covers.

1. What is something you have hidden before?
2. Why do people try to hide the bad things they do?
3. What are ways to uncover the bad things people do?

> *Dear God,*
> *Please help me never to cover up bad things. Show me how to do good things and live for you each day. Amen.*

Work Hard
EPHESIANS 6:6-7

Don't work only when your master is watching.
For then you will be lazy when he isn't looking.
Work hard and with gladness all the time. Do
everything as if you are working for Christ.

EPHESIANS 6:6-7

Everywhere you look, there is work to be done. Your dad wants you to clean your room. Your mom wants you to clean your plate. A schoolteacher wants you to hand out papers. A teacher at church asks for help straightening chairs. A friend asks for help picking up toys. Whenever there is work to be done, work hard and don't complain. It may be your mom or dad or teacher giving you the job. But Jesus is your REAL boss!

1. What jobs do you like to do? Why?
2. What jobs do you NOT like to do? Why?
3. Who is the best worker you know?

Dear God,
I don't want to be lazy. Help me to do all my work just for you. Amen.

When You're Scared
PHILIPPIANS 4:6

Don't worry about anything. Instead, pray about everything. Tell God your needs, and don't forget to thank him for his answers.

PHILIPPIANS 4:6

*B*ump! "What was THAT?" Paul was in a dark jail. Strange noises were all around him every night. He wrote this verse while he was in jail. "Pray. Do not worry," he wrote. The jail must have been a scary place for Paul. But God brought him peace. Praying made Paul feel safe. Remember to pray when you are afraid at night. Tell God each fear you have, one by one. Soon you will go to sleep.

1. What are you afraid of at night or in the dark?
2. How can you feel safe when you are afraid of the dark?
3. What words would you say to God when you're scared?

Dear God,
Thank you for watching over me each night. Remind me to pray when I am afraid. Amen.

Appreciation
1 Thessalonians 3:12

May the Lord make your love grow and overflow to each other. And may you love everyone else, just as we love you.

1 THESSALONIANS 3:12

Sometimes moms and dads get tired. Sometimes brothers and sisters get grumpy. When people in your family get tired and grumpy, see if you can cheer them up. Tell them you APPRECIATE them. Tell your mom, "I'm glad that you _____" (tell her what she does that makes you glad). Tell your dad, "I'm glad because you _____." Say to your sister or brother, "I'm glad you're in our family because _____." Then your love will overflow!

1. How do you feel when people tell you why they like you?
2. What do you appreciate most about your family members?
3. Who is one family member you can appreciate today?

Dear Lord,
    Thank you for everyone in my family. Please help me to appreciate them every day. Amen.

Praying for Friends

I direct you to pray much for others. Beg for God's mercy on them. Give thanks for all he is going to do for them.

1 TIMOTHY 2:1

Have you ever had a friend who was sad or scared? What about a friend who was sick? God says to pray for your friends. Your friends need your prayers. When you pray for your friends, you ask God to help them. You can pray for God to give them joy. You can pray for God to give them wisdom. You can even pray for God to heal them when they're sick. Pray for your friends. Maybe they're praying for you!

1. Who is a friend you have prayed for before?
2. What kinds of things can you pray to God about?
3. What happens when you pray to God?

Dear Lord,
*   Please remind me always to pray for my friends. Thank you for being my friend and listening to my prayers. Amen.*

Don't let anyone think little of you because you are young. Be their example. Let them follow the way you teach and live. Be a pattern for them in your love, your faith, and your clean thoughts.

1 TIMOTHY 4:12

Timothy was a Christian. Timothy was also young. But even the adults thought he was neat because he loved God. He did what God said, and everybody noticed. Timothy did loving things for people. Timothy trusted God. Timothy thought good, clean thoughts. By living this way, Timothy set an example for others. You can be a good example, too, just like Timothy—even if you're little!

1. What does it mean to be a good example?
2. What will other people do if you're a good example?
3. How can you be like Timothy today?

Dear God,
Thank you for teaching me about Timothy. Please help me to set a good example every day. Amen.

Money
1 TIMOTHY 6:9-10

People who long to be rich do all kinds of wrong things for money. They do things that hurt them and make them evil-minded. . . . The love of money is the first step toward all kinds of sin.

1 TIMOTHY 6:9-10

Do you have any money? Money is nice to have. You can buy things with it. But God warns us not to love it. "Who could love a dollar bill?" you might ask. Some people love money by thinking about it all the time. Others keep it all to themselves and don't share. Be thankful to God for the money you have. But don't love it. Save your love for God and other people.

1. What people in books or movies have loved money?
2. What bad things can happen to people who love money?
3. What is money good for?

Dear God,
    Thank you for money. Teach me to use it well but not to love it. Amen.

Talk about God
2 Timothy 1:5

I know how much you trust the Lord. You trust him just as your mother, Eunice, and your grandmother, Lois, do. I feel sure you are still trusting him as much as ever.

2 TIMOTHY 1:5

Timothy was a fine young man. He loved God and led his church. But how did he get to be like that? Here's the answer: He talked about God with his mother and grandmother. Next time you have a question about God, say, "Let's talk about God!" Then say what you know, and ask them what they know. You will have a fine talk that both of you will remember for a long time.

1. When was the last time you talked about God with your mom or dad?
2. What would you like to tell your grandmother or grandfather about God?
3. Among all the adults you know, who knows the most stuff about God?

Dear God,
*   You are more important to me than sports teams or toys or anything else. Please help me talk about you a lot. Amen.*

Think Before You Speak
JAMES 3:5-6

The tongue is a small thing. But what huge damage it can do. A great forest can be set on fire by one tiny spark.

JAMES 3:5

James was a down-to-earth person. "If you love God, then try to please him," he said. So his letter is full of good ideas for living as a Christian. James wrote some strong words about a small but important thing—the tongue! Angry words can really hurt people. When you are very angry, it is best not to say anything until you have calmed down a little. It is OK to be angry. Just stop and think before you say something you'll feel bad about later.

1. How do you feel when somebody yells at you?
2. When was the last time you said angry words to somebody?
3. What is a good way to tell some one they made you angry?

Dear God,
*   When I'm angry, please help me to think before I speak. Don't let me say angry words that really sting. Amen.*

Admit It When You're Wrong
JAMES 5:16

Tell each other when you do wrong. Pray for each other. Then you will be healed.

JAMES 5:16

Nobody is perfect. Everybody does bad things. Even good people sometimes do bad things. It's no fun to say, "I was wrong. I'm sorry." It's no fun to admit it when you do wrong. But it's a great thing to do, because then your mom and dad can forgive you. They can pray for you. They can hug you and say, "It's OK. I forgive you."

1. What happens in your family if you admit you did wrong instead of waiting to get caught?
2. If you were a parent, how would you talk with your child who just said, "I took a cookie without asking"?
3. How does telling someone about a sin keep you from doing it next time?

Dear God,
  Thank you for forgiving me when I sin. Help me to tell Mom or Dad when I do wrong so they can forgive me, too. Amen.

A Verse about Family
1 Peter 3:8

You should be like one big family. You should be full of kindness toward each other. Love one another with tender hearts and humble minds.

1 PETER 3:8

God wants your family to be a happy family. What makes a family happy? Families that love one another with tender hearts are happy. Happy families forgive each other. Happy families also help each other out. What kind of family do you want to be in? You can make your family happy by helping everyone. You can be patient and kind with your brothers and sisters. You can share God's love with your family. That will surely make them happy.

1. How does it help when someone is full of kindness toward another family member?
2. What makes you happy about your family?
3. Who is someone in your family you can help today? How?

Dear God,
Thank you for my family. Please help me to be kind and tenderhearted with all my family members. Amen.

Books were opened, including the Book of Life. And the dead were judged according to the things written in the books. Each one was judged according to the deeds he had done.

REVELATION 20:12

You can read more about heaven on page 418 of *The Eager Reader Bible*.

W hat will heaven be like?" people ask. We don't know everything about it. But this we do know: Heaven will be wonderful. And it will be for everyone who loves God. It will be for all the people who trust in Jesus. Do you know any people who love God? Don't be shy—copy them. Trust in Jesus like they do. Listen to their advice. You'll be glad you did.

1. Who sometimes copies what you do? (Hint: A little brother or sister? A pet? A friend?)
2. Which of your friends love God and trust in Jesus?
3. What's one thing you can copy from somebody who loves God?

Dear God,
Thank you for all the people who love you and will someday be in heaven with you. Please help me to learn from them. Amen.

No More Tears
REVELATION 21—22

[God] will wipe away all tears from their eyes. There shall be no more death, sorrow, crying, or pain. All of that has gone forever.

REVELATION 21:4

The story of what heaven will be like starts on page 418 of *The Eager Reader Bible*.

Heaven is very, very different from earth. In heaven, nothing will ever make you sad. No one will ever get hurt or die. You'll never have tears running down your cheeks or a drippy nose. You'll never scrape your knee again. Bees won't sting you ever again. When you feel sad, think about heaven. It's the most wonderful place you could ever be. Heaven is a very special place. God made heaven for you and everyone who loves God.

1. What kinds of things make you sad?
2. What do you like to do when you're happy?
3. What is one thing you want to do in heaven?

Dear God,
   Thank you for making heaven a very special place for me. When I'm sad, please help me to think about heaven again. Amen.

TOPICAL INDEX

SCRIPTURE INDEX